CAMBODIA
in Pictures

VGS

Margaret J. Goldstein

Lerner Publications Company

Contents

Lerner Publishing Group realizes that current information and statistics quickly become out of date. To extend the usefulness of the Visual Geography Series, we developed www.vgsbooks.com, a website offering links to up-to-date information, as well as in-depth material, on a wide variety of subjects. All of the websites listed on www.vgsbooks.com have been carefully selected by researchers at Lerner Publishing Group. However, Lerner Publishing Group is not responsible for the accuracy or suitability of the material on any website other than <www.lernerbooks.com>. It is recommended that students using the Internet be supervised by a parent or teacher. Links on www.vgsbooks.com will be regularly reviewed and updated as needed.

Website address: www.lernerbooks.com

Lerner Publications Company
A division of Lerner Publishing Group
241 First Avenue North
Minneapolis, MN 55401 U.S.A.

web enhanced @ www.vgsbooks.com

Library of Congress Cataloging-in-Publication Data

Taus-Bolstad, Stacy.
    Cambodia in pictures / by Stacy Taus-Bolstad.
      p. cm. – (Visual geography series)
    Includes bibliographical references and index.
    Contents: The land – History and government – The people – Cultural life – The economy.
    ISBN: 0-8225-1994-1 (lib. bdg. : alk. paper)
    1. Cambodia–Juvenile literature. [1. Cambodia.] I. Title. II. Series.
DS554.3.T38 2004
959.6–dc22   2003019639

Manufactured in the United States of America
1 2 3 4 5 6 - BP - 09 08 07 06 05 04

INTRODUCTION

The Kingdom of Cambodia (known to Cambodians as Kampuchea) is a small, lush nation in Southeast Asia. In its long history, dating back thousands of years, the country has experienced both splendor and horror. Starting in the ninth century A.D., Cambodian kings built the magnificent city of Angkor, which remains to this day filled with grand temples and sculptures. In the twentieth century, Cambodia was ruled by one of the most brutal regimes in history, the Khmer Rouge, a group that murdered millions of Cambodians. In the early twenty-first century, Cambodia is trying to rebuild after decades of war and destruction. Although it is a poor nation economically, it is culturally and historically rich. Its story begins in ancient times.

Ancient Cambodia was home to several different ethnic groups. Most people lived in villages and farms on the level and fertile plain of central Cambodia. Rice cultivation became the basis of their economy. The first large, organized state in Cambodia was Funan,

which arose in the first century A.D. Traders sailing from India brought new political systems, art forms, and religious practices to Funan.

The Khmer, the country's largest ethnic group, arrived in Cambodia from southern China more than two thousand years ago. Khmer civilization reached its peak in the ninth century, when Khmer kings ruled a powerful empire. Its capital was the vast city of Angkor in the modern-day province of Siem Reap. During the Angkor period, Khmer authority and culture spread into neighboring Laos, Thailand, and Vietnam.

The Khmer Empire began to decline in the fourteenth century, as hostile neighbors overran Cambodian territory. Angkor's glorious temples were abandoned. Overshadowed by the powerful realms of its neighbors, Cambodia continued to shrink in size and importance. It came under French control in 1863. After occupation by Japan during World War II (1939–1945), Cambodia won its independence in 1954.

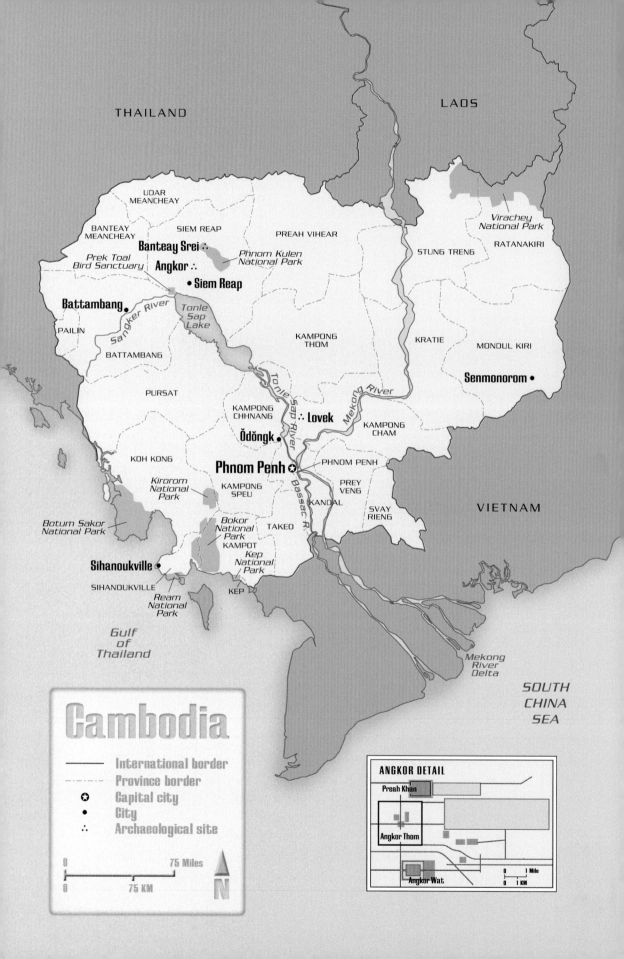

Cambodia was relatively peaceful in the 1950s and 1960s. It remained neutral as a war between Communists and non-Communists raged in neighboring Vietnam. But in 1970, members of the Cambodian military seized power from the prime minister. Then, in 1975, Cambodian Communists, called the Khmer Rouge, overran the capital of Phnom Penh and took over the government.

Under their leader, Pol Pot, the Khmer Rouge forced people to leave Cambodia's cities and to live at rural work camps and farms. Several million Cambodian citizens were executed or died of starvation or disease during the Khmer Rouge era. Vietnam invaded Cambodia in 1978 and installed a pro-Vietnamese government to replace the Khmer Rouge. Under international pressure, Vietnam withdrew its troops in 1989.

In 1993 elections supervised by the United Nations brought a new government to Cambodia. But political strife continued. Well into the 1990s, Khmer Rouge fighters still attacked government forces in isolated regions of the country.

Finally, in the late 1990s, Cambodia established a stable government. The Khmer Rouge was at last brought down. People rebuilt their schools and homes. They replanted their fields with crops and went back to work. Despite ongoing economic, political, and social struggles, Cambodians have become hopeful for a prosperous and peaceful future.

Cambodia is busy **rebuilding** its war-torn cities.

THE LAND

Roughly circular in shape on a map, Cambodia is located on the Indochinese Peninsula in Southeast Asia. The country's neighbors include Thailand to the west and northwest, Laos to the northeast, and Vietnam to the east and southeast. With a total land area of 69,898 square miles (181,000 square kilometers), Cambodia is about the size of the state of North Dakota. The country's greatest distance from north to south is 280 miles (451 km). From east to west, Cambodia stretches 350 miles (563 km).

Topography

Cambodia has two main geographical regions: the low-lying Central Cambodian Plain in the central and southeastern part of the country and a ring of mountains to the west and north plus highlands in the east. The plain includes the large freshwater Tonle Sap Lake in the west-central part of the country. The land around the lake is shaped like a large, shallow basin. It is wet and marshy. Reeds and tall

grasses grow in the basin's rich soil. This area is home to 85 percent of the country's people. Most of them are farmers who grow rice or catch fish from the basin's rivers and lakes.

Cambodia's highlands include the Dangrek Mountains, along the northern border with Thailand, and the Elephant and Cardamom Mountains in the southwest. Cambodia's highest peak—Mount Aôral—reaches an elevation of 5,947 feet (1,813 meters) in the sparsely populated Cardamom range. Pines and other evergreen trees grow on the tallest hills and mountains. Tropical rain forests grow at lower elevations. Cambodia has a rugged, 200-mile (322-km) coastline. It faces the Gulf of Thailand, an arm of the South China Sea.

◉ Rivers and Lakes

Cambodia is a naturally well watered country, crisscrossed by large and small rivers. When rainfall is heavy, the rivers sometimes flood.

THAILAND

LAOS

DANGREK MOUNTAINS

Khone Falls

Sangker River

Tonle
Sap
Lake

CENTRAL
CAMBODIAN
PLAIN

Tonle Sap River

Mekong River

Bou Sraa Waterfall

CARDAMOM
MOUNTAINS

▲
Mount
Aôral

Bassac R.

ELEPHANT
MOUNTAINS

VIETNAM

Gulf
of
Thailand

Mekong
River
Delta

Cambodia

Feet	Meters	
9843	3000	Mountains
6582	2000	Uplands
3281	1000	Lowlands
1640	500	

Elevation

N

―――― International border
▲ Mountain peak

0   75 Miles
0   75 KM

SOUTH
CHINA
SEA

For centuries, Cambodia's rice farmers have used irrigation, a system of reservoirs and canals, to divert water from the nation's rivers to their fields. The rivers are also an important source of freshwater fish.

Cambodia's major waterway is the Mekong River, which begins far to the northwest in the mountains of Tibet (an autonomous region of China). The Mekong enters Cambodia at Khone Falls on the Laotian border. Carrying vast amounts of fertile soil downstream, the Mekong gradually widens as it runs south through Cambodia. The river bottom is rocky, creating dangerous rapids that make it impossible for boats to travel very far upriver.

At Phnom Penh, the nation's capital city, the Mekong is joined by the Tonle Sap River, which flows south from the lake of the same name. The Mekong then divides into two branches. The lower branch, the Bassac River, runs through southeastern Cambodia and southern Vietnam, emptying into the South China Sea. The upper branch, which keeps the name Mekong, splits into six smaller waterways before reaching Vietnam's seacoast. (The area where the rivers meet the sea is called the Mekong River delta.) Many smaller rivers run through Cambodia, feeding into the Mekong, the Tonle Sap Lake, or the Tonle Sap River.

During Cambodia's annual rainy season, the Mekong floods and rises. The rising river water backs up from the Mekong into the Tonle Sap River, which in turn backs up into the Tonle Sap Lake. This backup of water causes the lake to grow in size from 1,000 square

A car ferry concludes a trip across the **Mekong River.** The name Mekong comes from the Thai name for the river, Mae Nam Khong, or "Mother of the Waters." At 2,600 miles (4,200 km) long, the Mekong is the seventh longest river in Asia and the twelfth longest in the world.

miles (2,590 sq. km) to more than 6,000 square miles (15,540 sq. km), with its depth increasing from 3 feet (1 m) to 27 feet (9 m). In the dry season, the waters recede, draining back into the Tonle Sap River and downstream into the Mekong.

HOUSES ON STILTS

For thousands of years, Cambodians have built wooden houses on stilts—sometimes more than 9 feet (3 m) off the ground. Building houses this way allows homes to stay dry during the rainy season, when lakes and rivers often flood. When the land is flooded, people travel from house to house in small boats. Rural Cambodians have always built their houses with natural materials, such as bamboo, palm leaves, and rattan. This practice continues into modern times. In the cities, however, people build houses with many different materials, such as concrete, wood, brick, and stone.

◎ Climate

Cambodia has a tropical climate, which means it is always hot and humid and often rainy. From May through October, rain-bearing winds called monsoons blow across Southeast Asia from the southwest, bringing moisture from the Indian Ocean. The southern coast of Cambodia—the wettest part of the country—receives 100 inches (254 centimeters) or more of rain each year, most of it during the summer monsoon.

Another monsoon blows from the northeast from November to March. Coming from the South China Sea, the winter monsoon is milder than the summer monsoon, and the winter monsoon brings less moisture. Much of the rain falls on northern Vietnam before reaching Cambodia. As a result, the winter months in Cambodia are drier than the summer season. In some years, the dry season stretches on for months without rain, leaving the terrain brown and cracked.

Some Cambodians live in homes built on stilts to protect them in case there is a flood.

Average temperatures in Cambodia vary by only a few degrees throughout the year. Thermometer readings rarely fall below 70°F (21°C) in low-lying areas or below 50°F (10°C) in the highlands. The hottest month of the year is April, when temperatures can reach 85°F (30°C). In Phnom Penh, the temperature averages about 80°F (27°C) year-round. Destructive rainstorms called typhoons occasionally rake Southeast Asia. These storms often hit Vietnam's coastal areas hard, then die down before reaching Cambodia.

Flora and Fauna

In the mid-1900s, Cambodia was more than 70 percent forested. By the end of the century, with vast amounts of woodlands logged for lumber and firewood, that figure had been reduced to 30 percent. Despite the extensive logging, broad-leaved evergreen trees still cover the highest hills and mountains of the north, while pines and deciduous (leaf-shedding) trees grow in other hilly areas. Thick tropical rain forests grow at lower elevations.

Many different trees and plants grow in Cambodia. Pines and other evergreen trees grow at the highest elevations. Thick tropical rain forests grow at lower altitudes. The central plain features tall grasses and reeds, while the coast has tangled mangroves, vines, rattans, palms, bamboos, and other woody plants. Cambodians harvest wild bread-fruits, jackfruits, mangoes, papayas, bananas, and other fruits for food.

Cambodia's mountains, plains, and forests are home to a variety of animal life. Herons, cranes, pelicans, cormorants, egrets, and wild ducks flock to Cambodia's wetlands, while grouse, pheasants, and peacocks take refuge in the prairie grasslands.

A **breadfruit tree** can grow up to 60 feet (19 m) tall. Individual fruits weigh up to 10 pounds (4.5 kg).

The country has many species of snakes. Several of them—including the king cobra and the Russell's viper—are poisonous. The gecko, a small lizard, lives in or near many Cambodian homes. Geckos devour insects but seldom bother humans.

Cambodia has hundreds of varieties of saltwater and freshwater fish. Catfish larger than adult humans swim alongside carp, lungfish, and perch in the Mekong River. Fishers net tiny smelts from smaller rivers and lakes, as well as frogs, freshwater prawns (similar to shrimp), and turtles.

Mammals such as tigers, bears, panthers, wild oxen, deer, and small monkeys live in sparsely populated regions. Asian elephants survive in the rural north and northeast. However, many of these mammals are endangered, or threatened with extinction. They have become increasingly rare in Cambodia due to illegal hunting and habitat loss.

Natural Resources

Farmland has always been Cambodia's most important natural resource. The most heavily farmed regions are the Tonle Sap basin and the major river valleys. Rice is Cambodia's major crop. Other agricultural products include corn, oranges, soybeans, rubber, and coconuts. Many Cambodian farmers practice aquaculture, or fish farming, along rivers. These farmers raise catfish and other species in artificial ponds.

Cambodia's rain forests, perhaps the nation's most valuable natural resource, are in serious decline, as thousands of trees are cut each year and sold abroad. Intensive logging began in the late 1960s and continues at an aggressive pace. The most valuable trees are hardwoods such as teak and mahogany, which can grow to heights of more than 100 feet (30 m). Smaller trees such as bamboo, sugar palms, and rattan palms grow beneath the larger ones.

Deposits of iron ore, manganese ore, and gold are found in central and northern Cambodia. Limestone, a useful building material, is found in southern Cambodia. The south also has rocks containing phosphate, a chemical used to make fertilizer. Rubies, sapphires, and other precious stones are mined in the western part of the country. Coal deposits have been found in central and northern Cambodia.

People search for gemstones in the municipality (large urban area) of Pailin.

In the 1990s, oil and gas deposits were found offshore, in the Gulf of Thailand. Drilling there is expected to yield large reserves. The country's rivers also have enormous potential for hydroelectricity—energy created from the power of rushing water. Several hydroelectric stations already operate on the nation's small rivers, with more planned for the Mekong.

▶ Environmental Issues

Cambodia faces several serious environmental problems. One of the most critical is excessive logging of its rain forests. In the mid-1900s, Cambodia was more than 70 percent forested. By the end of the century, that figure had dropped to 30 percent. According to an international environmental protection group called Rainforest Action Network, Cambodia's rain forests are shrinking at a rate of 2 percent per year—twice the worldwide rate.

People have cut down Cambodia's rain forests for their valuable timber, which is sold around the world. But Rainforest Action Network and other groups charge that the Cambodian government does not properly manage the nation's forests. For instance, the government places few restrictions on logging and has not implemented reforestation—the planting of new trees to replace those that have been cut. In addition, many Cambodian loggers operate illegally, ignoring laws and cutting down forests that are supposed to be off-limits to logging. Much of the illegal cutting takes place along the Thai border, where loggers can quickly haul the felled trees out of the country.

Tamed Asian elephants carry tourists and other loads in Cambodia. Wild populations of the elephant are endangered.

As rain forests are cut, forest animals have fewer places to live. With their natural homes destroyed, many animals cannot survive. A number of Cambodian animals are endangered. Endangered species include Asian elephants, Asiatic wild dogs, leopards, wild oxen, tigers, rhinoceroses, and water buffalo. Many kinds of birds, bats, tortoises, fishes, snakes, and crocodiles are also endangered.

People need the rain forests too. For instance, rural Cambodians burn fallen trees for heating and cooking fuel. They build homes out of rattan and bamboo. They make medicine out of tree leaves and bark. Forest plants and animals also provide people with food such as fruits, roots, and meat. The widespread cutting of forests means that Cambodian people have fewer forest products to use in their day-to-day lives.

Cutting down rain forests leads to other environmental problems. Where the forests have been cut, there are no tree roots left to hold the soil in place. Soil washes away in rainstorms. Hillsides turn muddy. Fields and irrigation ditches fill up with mud, and rainwater floods low-lying areas.

To protect rain forests and plant and animal species, the Cambodian government has set aside approximately 20 percent of the nation's land as Kirorom, Bokor, Kep, Ream, Botum Sakor, Phnom Kulen, and Virachey national parks plus numerous wildlife preserves, and other reserved areas. These areas are off-limits to loggers, hunters, and builders. However, the Cambodian government does not have a lot of money. It is not always able to fully staff the parks or to enforce regulations. Sometimes, loggers and hunters operate in the parks illegally, further destroying the plants and animals that live there.

On the positive side, since the country has become more peaceful, more and more tourists are starting to visit Cambodia. Many tourists visit parks and preserves. They enjoy Cambodia's natural wonders, ancient ruins, and exotic animals. Called ecotourists, these nature-loving visitors bring much-needed money to Cambodia. They also help increase awareness of environmental issues. The money tourists spend in Cambodia might help the government protect endangered species, better staff parks and preserves, and crack down on illegal hunting and logging.

Cities

Most Cambodians live in small, rural villages or on farms. In fact, only about 15 percent of the nation's 12.7 million people live in urban areas. The nation has just a few big cities.

PHNOM PENH Lying in southeastern Cambodia, Phnom Penh is Cambodia's capital. It is also the nation's largest city, with a population of approximately 1 million people. It sprawls along the banks of three rivers—the Mekong, the Tonle Sap, and the Bassac.

The city's history dates to the 1430s, when the Khmers abandoned Angkor, their original capital north of Tonle Sap Lake. Rulers chose Phnom Penh as their new capital city. The site offered a good river port, with an outlet to the South China Sea through Vietnam. From Phnom Penh, Khmer traders could travel by boat to China, Laos, Vietnam, and other Asian nations. The city thrived and then declined. In the 1500s, a Khmer king moved the capital to Lovek, north of Phnom Penh. In 1772 invading Thai forces burned Phnom Penh to the ground.

The city was rebuilt, but it continued to struggle until the French took control of Cambodia in 1863. In 1867 Phnom Penh became the nation's capital once again. The French filled the city with grand buildings and boulevards. Businesses thrived, and the city's population grew steadily. During the conflicts of the late twentieth century, however, the capital fell into ruins. In 1975 the Khmer Rouge evacuated the city and left its buildings to decay in the hot, humid climate.

A *wat* is a Buddhist temple or monastery. **Wat Phnom,** built in 1372, stands in Phnom Penh. It is built on a man-made 89-foot (27-m) hill. Visit vgsbooks.com for links to websites with additional information about Phnom Penh, Sihanoukville, Battambang, and Siem Reap, including climate information and weather forecasts.

When peace returned in the 1980s and 1990s, Phnom Penh saw yet another revival. Those who had survived the brutal Khmer Rouge regime returned to their homes and office buildings. Foreign investors and tourists arrived to take part in the city's renewal. Businesspeople opened dance clubs, restaurants, and theaters. Some residents renovated impressive buildings from the French era. Roads and sewers were repaired. New parks and walkways were built along the city's riverfront. Phnom Penh is once again a bustling urban center. But like many big cities, it has great gaps between rich and poor. While parts of the city are flourishing, other areas are run-down and impoverished.

SIHANOUKVILLE Sihanoukville was named for King Norodom Sihanouk, who ruled in the mid-twentieth century and became king again in 1993. With a population of 155,000, Sihanoukville is the second largest city in Cambodia. Located on the Gulf of Thailand, it is a leading resort area, filled with hotels, nightclubs, and restaurants. The city has had a short history. It was created in the late 1950s to serve as a deepwater port on the ocean. Tourists began to arrive in the 1960s but disappeared as military conflicts increased throughout the nation. With the overthrow of Sihanouk (then prime minister) in 1970, the town's name was changed to Kampong Som (meaning "Port beneath the Moon"). As hostilities died down in the 1980s, tourists began to return. The city regained its former name in 1993. Increasingly popular, Sihanoukville boasts beautiful white sand beaches, nearby parks and waterfalls, and picturesque offshore islands. Wealthy Cambodians flock there from Phnom Penh on weekends.

This white sand beach graces an island in the **Gulf of Thailand** near Sihanoukville.

Scaffolding surrounds **an imposing statue of the Buddha** in Battambang.

BATTAMBANG Battambang is next in size with about 140,000 inhabitants. Located in western Cambodia, the city lies on the Sangker River, about halfway between the Tonle Sap Lake and the Thai border. Established in the tenth century, Battambang became part of Thailand in the late 1700s. The city rejoined Cambodia in the early 1900s. Like all Cambodians, Battambang residents suffered greatly under the Khmer Rouge regime. In the 1990s, as peace returned to Cambodia, the city began its revival.

Battambang is a transportation hub. A national highway runs through the city, as does a railroad line. Boat service runs along the Sangker River between Battambang and the nearby city of Siem Reap. An active commercial city, Battambang is an important transfer point for timber and other goods traded between Cambodia and Thailand. The city features attractive French-era buildings. It is also a starting point for tourists exploring ruins in the area, especially the ancient monuments of Angkor.

SIEM REAP Siem Reap is a town in the northwest, close to Angkor. Many of its 85,000 residents support themselves by catering to tourists. They work in hotels and restaurants and guide visitors to the temples and monuments of Angkor. Street vendors offer souvenirs from Angkor, including rubbings of images carved into the stone temples and replicas of ancient musical instruments, crossbows, and knives. Siem Reap is a mixture of old and new. French-colonial-era buildings here mingle with new luxury tourist hotels. Like Battambang, the city was controlled for a time by Thailand.

HISTORY AND GOVERNMENT

Archaeologists have found tools, pots, and other artifacts at many ancient sites in Cambodia. These objects indicate that the region has been inhabited for at least six thousand years. The identity of the earliest settlers is unknown, however. They may have been Australoids—people who migrated northward from Australia by boat, eventually reaching Southeast Asia.

People from South Pacific island groups later moved into Cambodia. These groups may have been fleeing enemies, searching for better hunting grounds, or looking to raise crops and livestock in more fertile fields and pastures. By about 200 B.C., the Khmer had migrated to the area from southern China. The ancestors of modern-day Cambodians, the Khmer were at first just one of many ethnic groups in the region.

The Khmer and other early peoples settled near the Tonle Sap Lake and along the Mekong River. They lived in wooden houses raised on stilts above the surrounding marshy land. They made tools, weapons,

and urns out of bronze and other metals. For food, they caught fish, grew rice, and raised pigs and water buffalo. They practiced ancient traditional religions, which were based on ancestor worship and spirit worship.

The First Kingdom

The first kingdom—an organized state headed by a monarch—in the area that would later become Cambodia was called Funan. Established in the first century A.D., it grew to become one of the most powerful kingdoms in early Southeast Asia. Historians are not sure of the kingdom's boundaries, but it probably included much of Southeast Asia. Its capital, Vyadhapura, was located in southeastern Cambodia.

Traders from ancient India had a strong influence on Funan. Arriving from the west, Indian ships stopped in the kingdom's ports to take on fresh food and water. Indian traders exchanged silk, iron, and bronze goods for valuable spices, gold, and ivory from Southeast Asia. Many Indians settled permanently in Funan, spreading Indian art and ideas among the kingdom's upper classes.

The Indian traders and settlers followed the Buddhist and Hindu faiths, and these religions spread throughout Funan, as did Sanskrit, an ancient Indian language. Funan also adopted an Indian code of laws. Chandan, an Indian aristocrat, became king of Funan in A.D. 357.

Funan's farmers built large-scale irrigation systems, an idea that might also have come from India. Using a series of dikes and canals, farmers diverted the waters of the Mekong and Tonle Sap Rivers to their rice fields. Irrigation allowed farmers to bring previously unfertile lands under cultivation. Rice harvests increased—some farmers harvested rice three times a year.

Funan's small group of rulers and upper-class citizens grew rich and powerful. The kingdom's commoners were required to give their surplus rice harvests to the king, as well as tax payments in the form of jewelry, perfumes, and precious metals. Funan's rulers also demanded tribute, or payment, from smaller, less powerful kingdoms in Southeast Asia. With their riches, the ruling classes built impressive fortresses, palaces, and temples.

The common people, by contrast, worked long hours for meager earnings. Their lives were short and harsh. Ethnic minorities such as the Mon—tribal people in the northern highlands—were often forced into slavery. Many people suffered from diseases that spread easily, including malaria, tuberculosis, and typhus, for which doctors had no cures. Food poisoning and deadly snakebites occurred frequently.

◉ The Early Khmer Empire

In the seventh century, Chenla, a tribute-paying state to the north, revolted against Funan and took over the kingdom. By then, the Khmer people had grown to become the dominant ethnic group in the region. During the Chenla period, many small Khmer kingdoms rose and fell in the remote plains and highlands of Southeast Asia.

The carvings on this **temple door in Angkor** are made of sandstone.

A king named Jayavarman II assumed control of one such kingdom in 802. He set out to unify all the Khmer peoples in Southeast Asia. Jayavarman II established a single Khmer state known as Cambodia (called Kambuja or Kampuchea in Khmer, the language of the Khmer), named for the mythical founder of the Khmer people. A fervent follower of Hinduism, Jayavarman II proclaimed himself to be a "god-king." Late in the ninth century, after Jayavarman II's death, his successors founded a new city called Angkor, north of the Tonle Sap Lake. There they began building large, intricately designed monuments to honor the powerful empire that Jayavarman had established. With its elaborate complex of stone temples, Angkor instilled respect and fear among the neighbors of the Khmer, who saw the monuments as a sign of growing Khmer power. Angkor became the capital of Cambodia around 900. It continued to grow, as successive kings built additional temples there.

In the tenth and eleventh centuries, Khmer kings pushed westward into present-day Thailand. They built a more sophisticated irrigation system, with new reservoirs and canals. This system allowed Khmer farmers to produce large surpluses of rice, which in turn made

This temple in Angkor, **Baksei Chamkrong,** was built in the mid-900s by Havsavarman I, the first king to live in the new capital.

Cambodia one of the most prosperous states in Southeast Asia. The kings of Cambodia demanded complete obedience from their subjects. Commoners had to work the farms of wealthy landowners. Men had to serve in the king's army and to labor on temple, palace, and irrigation construction projects. A group of Hindu priests called Brahmans held high government jobs and served as advisers to the king. Several Brahmans acquired great power of their own and built temples to salute their own glory.

Suryavarman I, who reigned in the eleventh century, extended the Khmer realm farther westward into Thailand and eastward into Vietnam. But as the kingdom grew larger, it became more difficult to manage. The common people revolted against high taxes, which were levied to pay for the capital's opulent temples and monuments. Several royal families vied for power. Armies in Thailand and Burma (modern-day Myanmar) threatened the western borders of the Khmer state.

Early in the twelfth century, King Suryavarman II defeated rival states in Vietnam and Burma. He oversaw the building of Angkor Wat, a vast temple in Angkor dedicated to the Hindu god Vishnu. But after Suryavarman's death in 1150, internal conflicts again weakened the kingdom. Champa, a small state on the Vietnamese coast, took advantage of the strife and rebelled against the Khmer rulers. A Champa army overran the Angkor region in 1177. But a prince named Jayavarman took back control for the Khmer and became king.

Unlike the previous kings ruling from Angkor, Jayavarman practiced Buddhism instead of Hinduism. After assuming the throne as Jayavarman VII, he built a number of new temples, statues, and other structures at Angkor. They featured images of Gautama Buddha (the Indian philosopher who founded Buddhism), as well as Hindu gods, Khmer kings, and daily Khmer life. Writings on the monuments described Jayavarman's success in extending the Khmer Empire farther into Vietnam, Laos, Thailand, and Malaysia.

HEAVEN ON EARTH

The design of Angkor Wat, Angkor's most famous temple complex, reflects Hindu mythology. The central tower stands for Mount Meru, the center of the universe and the home of the gods, according to Hindu teaching. The temple ground is surrounded by a wall and moat, which symbolize the mountains and oceans that are said to surround Mount Meru. The temple's entryway represents the rainbow bridge—the link between heaven, the realm of the gods, and earth, the realm of mortals, in Hindu mythology.

This stone carving *(above)* illustrates the social rank of Khmer people by their size. Common workers and soldiers *(right)* appear smaller than the ruler's carriage driver *(center)*, but the ruler *(seated in the carriage, left)* is the largest of all. **Angkor Wat** *(right)* is full of detailed stone carvings such as the one above.

◉ The Empire Falls

Before the end of Jayavarman VII's reign, Cambodia began to weaken. Massive construction projects had strained the royal budget. Irrigation networks began to break down. Thai forces pushed the Khmer out of central Thailand and continued eastward into Cambodia. They raided Angkor in 1353 and again in 1431. With Angkor losing its glory, the Khmer abandoned the capital and built one to the south, on the site of modern Phnom Penh.

From their new capital, closer to the ocean and to trade routes, the Khmer came in contact with traders from China, Europe, and the Middle East. In the 1500s, the Khmer king Ang Chan moved the capital once again, this time to Lovek, north of Phnom Penh. Thriving trade in Lovek attracted settlers from China, Japan, the Malay Peninsula, the Middle East, and the European countries of Spain and Portugal. Merchants in the city bought and sold silk, cotton, ivory, precious stones, incense, and livestock.

The sixteenth century was a time of disorder within Cambodia. Thai and Vietnamese armies occupied parts of the kingdom, and Khmer rulers fought among themselves for power. A Khmer king named Sattha asked for military support from Spain, which was expanding its own power in Southeast Asia. But by the time Spanish soldiers arrived to help, in 1596, Thai forces had already captured Lovek.

While the Thai threatened the Khmer from the west, the Vietnamese approached from the east. Vietnamese forces pushed into the Mekong River delta, which was then populated by Khmer farmers. Greatly weakened, the Khmer king made an alliance with the Vietnamese around 1620. As part of this agreement, the Vietnamese won the right to settle in the Mekong River delta themselves. Vietnamese governors took control of trade and farming in the region. By the late 1700s, the delta was completely under Vietnamese control. The Khmer had lost access to the sea.

Spain, led by King Phillip II, tried to expand its power and territory into Southeast Asia.

As Cambodia grew weaker, the Thai grew more powerful. In 1794 Thailand took over several northern Cambodian provinces, including the provinces of Battambang and Siem Reap. Pressured by Vietnam in the east and Thailand in the west, Cambodia finally agreed to be ruled jointly by its two neighbors. Ang Duong, the brother of a former Khmer king, was named the new king of Cambodia. But in actuality, he was completely under foreign control.

French Colonization

Ang Duong sought assistance from France, a European nation that was also expanding its power in Southeast Asia. Duong wanted France's help in regaining lands lost to Vietnam. French leaders wanted a foothold in Cambodia to slow the expansion of Thailand, which had allied itself with Great Britain—France's European rival. The French government also sought to open a trade route along the Mekong River into China. (The French soon learned that large merchant ships could not navigate the rocky Mekong, however.)

A FRENCHMAN "DISCOVERS" ANGKOR

After Angkor was abandoned in the late 1400s, its grand sandstone temples began to erode. Massive trees grew up and over the monuments, covering them in roots. Thieves ran off with many of the city's sculptures, statues, and carvings. Although Cambodians and a few foreign travelers knew about the complex, for centuries it remained unknown to the outside world. Then, in 1860, a French naturalist named Henri Mouhot came upon Angkor while exploring the Cambodian jungle. He published a book about his "discovery" of Angkor, complete with vivid descriptions and color sketches of the temples. The book created an international sensation. Explorers, photographers, and tourists flocked to the site from all over the world.

Like Henri Mouhot forty years earlier, Lunet de Lajonquière, a French colonel stationed in Southeast Asia in the early 1900s, led many **expeditions to Angkor.** He identified more than 900 monuments of various sizes in the area.

In 1863 the French used military force to pressure the new Cambodian king, Norodom, into signing a treaty with France. The treaty allowed France to mine gems and other minerals in Cambodia and to harvest the nation's rich forests. In exchange, the French agreed to protect the king from the Thai army and from rebellions within his own realm. Under further pressure, Norodom signed another agreement in 1884. This agreement transformed Cambodia into a French colony— a region under mostly French control. France also established other colonies in Southeast Asia, including Vietnam and Laos.

The agreement with France was not advantageous to ordinary Cambodians. The French imposed a new agricultural system on the nation. Under this system, peasant farmers had to buy their own land rather than work the farms of wealthy landowners. To do so, the peasants had to borrow money and pay huge interest rates on the loans. The French colonial government also imposed large tax increases on the farmers. Khmer resentment of French power steadily rose. A brief rebellion in the mid-1880s failed to loosen French control, however.

Relations between King Norodom and the French colonizers grew increasingly strained. The French angered the king by allowing Thailand to keep the Battambang and Siem Reap Provinces, which Thailand had seized in the late 1700s. As French forces in Cambodia expanded, King Norodom's power weakened further. Many of his rivals in Cambodia allied with the French to gain an advantage in their own pursuit of power. In 1897 the French took over the Cambodian government almost completely, reducing the king's power to nearly nothing.

King Norodom (third from left) and a young relative go for a carriage ride. Two drivers seated up front and two servants, one seated on the back of the carriage and one following on horseback, accompany them.

In 1904 King Norodom died. He was succeeded by his half-brother, King Sisowath, who cooperated with the French and ruled peacefully for more than twenty years. During his reign, French negotiators convinced Thailand to return Battambang and Siem Reap to Cambodia.

During the 1920s, Cambodia built new roads and a railroad line. French colonial officials established rubber plantations (large farms) in eastern Cambodia and began restoring the long-neglected temples of Angkor. Rice and rubber were in great demand, and Cambodia benefited from selling these crops on the world market. Ordinary Cambodians did not benefit from this prosperity, however. The French labor system kept them virtually enslaved, unable to work their way out of debt. In 1927 peasants rebelled against the French-run labor and tax systems, but the Cambodian military quickly put down the protest.

Independence

During World War II (1939–1945), Japan, an Asian island nation, invaded and occupied much of Southeast Asia, including Cambodia. The Japanese government let the French continue to administer Cambodia and its Asian colonies, however. Although the Japanese largely let the French govern as they pleased, in 1941 they did force the French to give Battambang and Siem Reap back to Thailand (a Japanese ally).

When the next Cambodian king, Monivong, died in 1941, French

Like his father, King Sisowath, **King Monivong,** shown here wearing traditional ceremonial clothing, cooperated with the French. He ruled Cambodia from 1927 to 1941.

A solemn young man, **Prince Norodom Sihanouk** attends the funeral for his grandfather King Monivong. Sihanouk was nineteen years old when the French made him the next king of Cambodia.

officials placed Prince Norodom Sihanouk—Monivong's grandson—on the throne. Although the prince's father (the logical choice for king) was still alive, French officials believed they could more easily control the younger man. But King Sihanouk was an energetic and ambitious ruler who enjoyed widespread popularity among ordinary Cambodians. He sought to free Cambodia from foreign control and looked for an opportunity to fight for Cambodia's independence from France.

Sihanouk's chance came on March 9, 1945, when Japan dissolved the French government in Cambodia. Three days later, the king declared Cambodia's independence. But later that year, World War II ended with a Japanese surrender. With Japan defeated, France returned to power in Southeast Asia.

The Battambang and Siem Reap Provinces were again returned to Cambodia. But because France did not have enough money or troops to maintain control over these provinces, they were declared autonomous, or self-governing, zones. They enjoyed some freedom from French authority. Meanwhile, the brief period of independence in 1945 inspired many Cambodians to press for permanent independence. In 1946 France agreed to let the Cambodians elect a national assembly, or legislature, and write a constitution. The new government left the king, Sihanouk, in place, but his role in the government was unclear. In reality, France still held a lot of power in the country, especially in the areas of taxation, foreign policy, the court system, and the military.

The new Cambodian national assembly lacked experience. In addition, its leading members struggled with one another and with King Sihanouk for power. By 1953 King Sihanouk had dissolved the national assembly and taken over the government. He left the country briefly—traveling to France, the United States, and other nations—to drum up international support for Cambodian independence. Later that year, the French formally granted Cambodia its independence. Vietnam and Laos gained independence from France in 1954.

Seeking to gain more power, Sihanouk gave up the throne to his aging father, Norodom Suramarit, and became a private citizen—an

In a traditional coronation ceremony for King Norodom Suramarit *(seated, left)*, Hindu priests *(kneeling, right)* blow into conch shells.

action that allowed him to run for political office. He formed a new political party called the People's Socialist Community Party, which won every seat in the Cambodian legislature in the 1955 elections. As the party's leader, Sihanouk became Cambodia's prime minister.

War in Southeast Asia

Meanwhile, Communists—people who favor a state-controlled economy, with no private property—were fighting to install a Communist government in newly independent Vietnam. As part of an international agreement, the nation was divided into North Vietnam and South Vietnam in 1954. A Communist government, backed by China and the Soviet Union, took charge in the north. A non-Communist government, backed by the United States, maintained control in the south. But there would be no peace between the two nations. With support from North Vietnam, the Viet Cong—a small band of Communist guerrillas (fighters who don't use traditional army tactics) based in the south—began attacking the South Vietnamese government. The fight between Vietnamese Communists and non-Communists eventually developed into the Vietnam War (1961–1975).

As Cambodia's prime minister, Norodom Sihanouk tried to maintain neutrality in the conflict. He feared the United States, which was an ally of both Thailand and South Vietnam (Cambodia's long-standing enemies). Yet he also mistrusted the North Vietnamese, who were helping Communist guerrillas inside Cambodia as well.

In 1965, after the U.S. government began sending combat troops to South Vietnam, Sihanouk broke off relations with the United States. He allowed the North Vietnamese and the Viet Cong to station troops within Cambodia. Many Cambodian officials, led by General Lon Nol, protested this policy. They favored ties with the United States and strongly opposed any agreement with the Communists.

With the aid of the United States, Lon Nol overthrew Sihanouk in March 1970. Sihanouk took refuge in China. Although initially popular, Nol lost the trust of the people when his army began killing Vietnamese living in Cambodia. At the same time, U.S. forces began illegally bombing eastern Cambodia, where the Viet Cong had built bases and supply routes. Though intended to damage the Viet Cong, the American bombs also killed thousands of Cambodian civilians. Hundreds of thousands more fled their homes to escape the destruction. The bombing lasted until 1973. It soon destroyed the Cambodian economy, leading to food shortages, high prices, and widespread hunger.

At the U.S. Embassy in Phnom Penh, **Cambodian citizens protest U.S. bombings** in Cambodia during the Vietnam War.

The Khmer Rouge Takes Over

Meanwhile, young Cambodians, many of whom had studied abroad, began organizing their own Communist groups. The Cambodian Communist movement became known as the Khmer Rouge, or Red Khmers (Communists in the early Soviet Union were also nicknamed Reds, after the color of their flag). Many Khmer Rouge fighters were trained by the Viet Cong.

The Communist message appealed to many ordinary Cambodians. They saw that their nation's leaders lived in wealth and splendor, while the common people were often poor and hungry. The Khmer Rouge promised to create a society in which everyone shared equally in the nation's wealth, with no distinctions between rich and poor. As they moved through the Cambodian countryside in the early 1970s, Khmer Rouge troops encouraged young villagers to join their movement. With the Cambodian economy in ruins and opposition to the Lon Nol government growing, many Cambodians took up arms with the Communists.

Under the leadership of a former Cambodian schoolteacher named Pol Pot, the Khmer Rouge waged war against the better equipped but poorly motivated Cambodian government armed forces. The Khmer Rouge received some assistance from the North Vietnamese and the Viet Cong, who were by then gaining the upper hand in South

Vietnam. In 1974 the Khmer Rouge overran the city of Ŏdŏngk, north of Phnom Penh, forcing the city's 20,000 citizens to flee. Those seen as a threat to Communist ideals—teachers, government employees, and intellectuals—were murdered. In the spring of 1975, the Khmer Rouge closed in on Phnom Penh itself, capturing the city on April 17. That same month, South Vietnam fell to North Vietnam, ending the Vietnam War.

Although Lon Nol's government had been unpopular, the Khmer Rouge regime was far worse. Under Pol Pot, the new prime minister, the new leaders renamed the country Democratic Kampuchea and established one of the most brutal and murderous governments in human history.

Pol Pot

The Khmer Rouge said they wanted to transform Cambodia into a Communist farming society, controlled by peasants. To institute their ideas, Khmer Rouge troops evacuated Phnom Penh and other cities and sent residents to forced-labor camps in the Cambodian countryside. Divided into work teams and supervised by brutal guards, people labored twelve to fifteen hours a day, clearing fields, planting crops, and digging irrigation canals. People who already lived in the countryside did not have to leave their villages. But the Khmer Rouge took over their farmlands and forced them, too, to perform backbreaking labor in the fields. At the rural work camps, no one could travel without permission. Everyone had to dress in peasant work clothing. Children were taken from their parents at age seven, housed in special children's units, and taught the Khmer Rouge Communist philosophy.

The Khmer Rouge planned to start society anew. They declared the first year of their regime, 1975, to be Year Zero. In the deserted cities, they closed down shops, schools, hospitals, and offices. Many banks, hotels, and Buddhist monasteries were blown up or burned down. The nation's money system was abolished, and mail delivery ceased. No books were allowed to be published.

The Khmer Rouge continued to arrest and execute people such as teachers, students, engineers, doctors, journalists, artists, the wealthy, and anyone associated with the Lon Nol government. Many victims were tortured before they were killed, then were buried in mass graves. At the forced labor camps, hundreds of thousands of Cambodians died of starvation, disease, and overwork. Historians believe that between one and four million people—or at least 15 percent of Cambodia's population—died under the Khmer Rouge regime. Few people were able to escape the nation during this period.

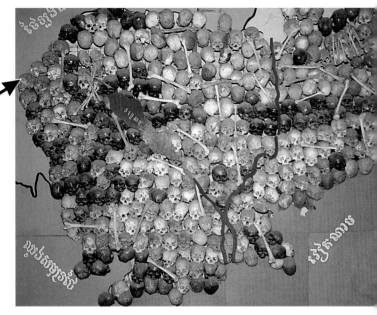

A Khmer Rouge map of Cambodia made of the skulls and bones of some Khmer Rouge victims is on display at the **Tuol Sleng Museum** in Phnom Penh. The museum is a former Khmer Rouge prison. Find reports on the Khmer Rouge at vgsbooks.com.

The Vietnamese Invasion

Although Khmer Rouge fighters had worked with Vietnamese Communists during the 1960s and early 1970s, Pol Pot later turned against the Vietnamese. Distrustful of Vietnam and fearful of its power, Pol Pot took action against the neighboring country beginning in 1976. First, he purged the Cambodian government of any officials who did not share his anti-Vietnamese sentiments—that is, he had these officials executed. By 1977 the Khmer Rouge army had invaded Vietnam, an act that eventually led to open warfare between the two nations.

In turn, Vietnam invaded Cambodia in December 1978. The Cambodian people had little motivation to defend the brutal Khmer Rouge and put up a feeble fight. The Vietnamese quickly captured Phnom Penh and set up a pro-Vietnamese Communist government there. The country was renamed the People's Republic of Kampuchea (PRK). Made up largely of pro-Vietnamese Cambodians who had deserted the Khmer Rouge, the PRK forced Pol Pot and his supporters into exile along the Thai border.

The new PRK regime reopened Cambodia's schools and hospitals and allowed city dwellers to return to their homes and some businesses to reopen. But these measures could not rescue the country's devastated economy. Because of warfare, very little rice was planted in 1979, and famine struck the nation that year. The United Nations sent food shipments to help relieve the famine. Most of the food never reached the hungry people, however, but instead was seized by opposing armies.

At the same time, hundreds of thousands of Cambodians fled their country for refugee camps in Thailand. Some refugees were former Khmer Rouge officials who feared the Vietnamese leadership. Others were ordinary citizens who feared the return of the Khmer Rouge.

In remote areas of the Cambodian countryside, various forces fought for control. These groups included supporters of Norodom Sihanouk and Lon Nol, both of whom had returned to Cambodia and were trying to regain power. Though weakened, the Khmer Rouge also remained active, carrying out guerrilla attacks in Cambodian towns, roads, and rice fields in an attempt to undermine Vietnamese control. Experts estimate that both the Khmer Rouge and the Vietnamese-backed government planted millions of landmines throughout the country, both to kill opposing forces and to

> After the Vietnamese took over, hundreds of thousands of Cambodians fled their nation. Although most of these refugees eventually returned to Cambodia, some made their way to other nations. Between 1975 and 1986, almost 150,000 Cambodian refugees moved to the United States, many settling in California, where they struggled to rebuild their lives and to adjust to life in a new country. They also mourned the families they had left behind in Cambodia—many of them murdered by the Khmer Rouge.

Landmine warning signs, such as this one, are still common throughout the Cambodian countryside. More than 40,000 Cambodians have lost limbs after accidentally exploding mines.

intimidate civilians. The mines eventually killed and injured thousands of ordinary Cambodians.

⊙ Self-Government Restored

Under international pressure, Vietnam withdrew its troops from Cambodia in 1989. In 1991 the Vietnamese-backed government agreed to step down and make way for a new government, to be elected by the Cambodian people. New political parties were formed: the anti-Communist Khmer People's National Liberation Front (KPNLF); Norodom Sihanouk's National United Front for an Independent, Neutral, Peaceful, and Cooperative Cambodia (FUNCINPEC); the Cambodian People's Party (CPP), with many members of the previous Communist government; and the Party of Democratic Kampuchea (PDK), led by the Khmer Rouge. The four groups agreed to a peace settlement and began negotiations to hold elections for a new Cambodian national assembly.

The United Nations organized a group called United Nations Transitional Authority in Cambodia (UNTAC) and sent peacekeeping troops and administrators to oversee the election, held in May 1993. Angered that the Vietnamese-affiliated CPP was allowed to participate, the PDK boycotted the election and tried to disrupt the voting process. Nevertheless, nearly 90 percent of Cambodians voted in the election, and a new national assembly was seated. FUNCINPEC and the CPP emerged as the leading parties in the assembly.

The assembly adopted a new constitution for Cambodia. It set up a

A NEW CONSTITUTION AND A NEW START

"We, the people of Cambodia; Accustomed to having been an outstanding civilization, a prosperous, large, flourishing and glorious nation, with high prestige radiating like a diamond; Having declined grievously during the past two decades, having gone through suffering and destruction, and having been weakened terribly; Having awakened and resolutely rallied and determined to unite for the consolidation of national unity, the preservation and defense of Cambodia's territory and precious sovereignty and the fine Angkor civilization, and the restoration of Cambodia into an "Island of Peace" based on multi-party liberal democratic responsibility for the nation's future destiny of moving toward perpetual progress, development, prosperity, and glory; With this resolute will; We inscribe the following as the Constitution of the Kingdom of Cambodia."

—Preamble to the Cambodian Constitution, 1993

King Norodom Sihanouk

type of government called a parliamentary monarchy—a government led by both a parliament, or legislature, and a king. The king's position, largely a ceremonial one, once again went to Norodom Sihanouk. The new government was supposed to have a single prime minister (the chief executive and the head of the leading party in the national assembly), but postelection turmoil led to fighting and then a compromise. The leading parties—FUNCINPEC and the CPP—agreed to appoint two prime ministers instead of one.

The Khmer Rouge was not content to give up power, however. From bases in the Cambodian countryside, it carried out guerrilla attacks against government and civilian targets. The government tried a number of tactics to root out the guerrillas, including offering them amnesty, or pardon, if they would fight their former Khmer Rouge colleagues on behalf of the government. Eventually, internal strife within the Khmer Rouge weakened the organization, and the government was able to drive thousands of its troops and supporters into Thailand. As stability returned, more than 350,000 refugees returned to Cambodia from camps in Thailand. In fits and starts, peace and safety began to return to Cambodia.

But the newly elected government struggled, largely due to disagreements between its two prime ministers, Hun Sen of the CPP and FUNCINPEC's Prince Norodom Ranariddh, the son of King Sihanouk. Each man built up a small security force, and in July 1997, Sen's troops attacked Ranariddh's troops. Ranariddh fled into exile but later returned. New elections were held in July 1998, and this time, the CPP won the most seats in the national assembly. Hun Sen became the nation's sole prime minister, but he agreed to share power with Ranariddh, whose FUNCINPEC Party had also made a strong showing in the election. Under the agreement, Ranariddh became president of the national assembly.

At peace for the first time in thirty years, Cambodia is finally starting to rebuild. Tourism is a growing industry, since the country has become relatively safe in recent years. Pol Pot was captured by former

Khmer Rouge fighters. He died in the Cambodian jungle on April 15, 1998 (the circumstances of his death are uncertain). By 1999 all of the remaining Khmer Rouge leaders had surrendered or been captured. At last, the nation is starting to look forward to a peaceful and secure future.

Government

The Cambodian national assembly consists of 122 members, elected by the people for five-year terms. All Cambodians over age eighteen have the right to vote. The national assembly makes laws for the nation and oversees areas of government such as finance, foreign affairs, and commerce. The prime minister, generally the leader of the party with the most seats in the national assembly, is the head of the executive branch of government. Cambodia also has a king, although this position is largely ceremonial—involving duties such as greeting foreign diplomats.

In 1998 the national assembly decided to create a sixty-one-member senate. The senate's main role is to review laws passed by the national assembly. Senators—some of whom are appointed, some elected by special interest groups—also serve five-year terms.

Cambodia has a judicial, or court, system made up of a supreme court and local courts. A body called the Constitutional Council hears court cases involving elections and constitutional issues. A group called the Supreme Council of Magistracy oversees the appointment and discipline of judges and prosecutors.

For matters of local government, the country is divided into twenty provinces and four municipalities (large urban areas), each administered by a governor. Provinces are further divided into districts, communes, and villages, with local leaders on these levels, many of them elected.

PUNISHMENT FOR THE KHMER ROUGE?

The international community—including the United Nations, the United States, and international human rights organizations—has called for tribunals, or trials, to bring former Khmer Rouge leaders to justice for the mass killings of millions of Cambodians. For several years, the United Nations and the Cambodian government could not agree on how trials should be carried out. Finally, in 2003 the United Nations approved a plan for holding the trials. The plan awaits ratification by the Cambodian national assembly.

THE PEOPLE

In 1998 the Cambodian government took its first census, an official count of the people, in decades. The population was estimated at 11.4 million in 1998 and 12.7 million in 2002. With an annual growth rate of 2.24 percent, that number is expected to reach 16.6 million by 2010. The bulk of the population is concentrated around the Tonle Sap Lake basin and the Mekong River valley. Most rural people are farmers. Only about 15 percent of the nation's people live in cities.

▶ Women, Children, and Family Life

In most Cambodian households, parents live together with their children, who remain in the home until they marry. The average Cambodian woman has four or five children during her lifetime. Grown children take in aging parents who can no longer care for themselves. Life expectancy is low: just 55 years for men and 60 years for women. Because few people live to old age and because

birth rates are high, the population is weighted toward the young. More than 40 percent of Cambodians are under the age of 15.

Because so many men were killed in warfare in the late 1900s, women outnumber men in the nation. In 2002 there were only 93 men for every 100 women, although the figures are coming back into balance as peace takes hold. Given the imbalance between numbers of men and women, it is not surprising that women head many households in Cambodia (one in five). However, women have not achieved prominence in public life, especially in the areas of business and government. Men hold most seats in the Cambodian national assembly. Few women serve as judges or hold other government jobs. Most professional and management positions are also held by men.

Traditionally, young women are discouraged from pursuing higher education or professional training. They are not allowed to study at Buddhist monasteries. Many girls end their schooling before high school. Many Cambodian women cannot read or write.

By law, Cambodian women have equal rights with men, but women still suffer many abuses in Cambodian society, such as domestic violence (physical abuse at the hands of family members). Some Cambodian families even sell their daughters into prostitution—the illegal sex trade. The Cambodian government and international human rights organizations have set out to protect girls and end child prostitution, but much work remains to be done.

Rural and Urban Life

Rural Cambodians live simply and often struggle to survive. Much of what they need, including food, fuel, building materials, and even medicine, comes from nearby forests, lakes, and rivers. Utilities such as electricity and telephone service are uncommon if not unknown in rural areas. Roads are unpaved, and many villagers have little contact with outsiders. Rainfall shortages and poor harvests have led to famine in years past. Decades of warfare have also hurt the farm economy. Many rural people survive with the help of food shipments from the United Nations and other international aid organizations.

Most Cambodian villages stretch along a road, river, or canal. Most have an open-air market, a few shops, a school, and a Buddhist temple. Stores are often constructed of stucco or cement. Most houses and schools are built of bamboo poles, with roofs

FASHION SENSE

Most Cambodian villagers wear sandals and loose cotton shirts. Both men and women wear baggy cotton trousers, while women sometimes wear skirts. Cambodians often wear colorful checkered scarves called *kramas*, usually worn around the head, neck, or shoulders. Both men and women sometimes wear sarongs—long strips of cloth wrapped around the body like a skirt or dress. Buddhist monks in Cambodia wear full-length orange robes. In the cities, many people wear Western-style clothing, such as T-shirts, blue jeans, and tennis shoes.

A young Cambodian villager wears a krama at an open-air market.

made of a thatch, or mat, of palm leaves. Many houses are built on stilts, as protection from flooding in the wet season. A few prosperous villagers have sturdier wooden houses with roofs made of tin or another metal. Small gardens, fruit and shade trees, and bushes adorn village homes. The typical village has several hundred inhabitants.

The traditional Cambodian greeting is the *sompiah*, which involves pressing the palms of the hands together and bowing. Some men use the Western handshake instead when greeting one another.

Most farming people leave their homes each morning after breakfast to plant, weed, or harvest in nearby agricultural fields. Other rural Cambodians work as fishers on nearby lakes or rivers. The laborers return home at noon to eat lunch, the largest meal of the day, then rest during the hottest midafternoon hours. After working again in the late afternoon, they prepare dinner. In many farming families, young children work alongside their parents in the fields.

Urban life is more varied and fast paced. Phnom Penh, the nation's capital, is a bustling city of about 1 million people. Its streets are filled with cars, bicycles, bicycle cabs called cyclos, motor scooters, and foot traffic. Street vendors crowd the sidewalks, selling everything from deep-fried spiders (a popular snack in Cambodia) to tourist souvenirs.

Phnom Penh has a growing supply of well-kept residential housing such as the homes in this neighborhood.

Beggars are also common—many of them amputees who lost their limbs to landmines. Urban buildings display a hodgepodge of architectural styles, from ancient palaces to French colonial mansions to brand-new luxury hotels to ramshackle wooden apartment houses.

People in Cambodian cities do a variety of jobs. They work in shops, banks, factories, and restaurants. Major urban industries include garment manufacturing, tourism, rubber and food processing, and cigarette manufacturing. Many city dwellers are part-time residents who leave for the countryside to plant rice during the wet season. Phnom Penh, Sihanoukville, Battambang, and other Cambodian cities are growing, as more and more young people move there from the countryside to look for jobs or to attend school. Tourists from Western countries will notice many familiar conveniences such as television, Internet cafés, and fast-food restaurants in Cambodian cities.

Ethnic Groups

The vast majority of Cambodians—around 90 percent—are Khmers. Their ancestors arrived in Cambodia from southern China more than two thousand years ago. Although the Khmers have long been the largest group in the nation, over the centuries, several other ethnic groups have moved into Cambodia. Traders and merchants from India, Java, and Malaysia began arriving in the eighth century A.D. Thai people immigrated from the tenth to fifteenth centuries A.D. Cham peoples—from the ancient kingdom of Champa in modern-day Vietnam—arrived after their defeat by the Vietnamese in the 1400s. Vietnamese people came in the seventeenth century, and Chinese arrived in the eighteenth and nineteenth centuries.

After taking power in 1975, the Khmer Rouge expelled or executed many minority groups in Cambodia. For the most part, only the Khmer remained, which accounts for their large proportion of the current population. In fact, Cambodia is the most ethnically uniform nation in Southeast Asia. Nevertheless, several ethnic minorities have survived. According to official government figures, Vietnamese make up 5 percent of the Cambodian population, Chinese make up 1 percent, and other ethnic groups account for 4 percent. But outside observers say that these percentages might actually be much higher.

Most Chinese Cambodians live in cities, where for centuries they have worked as merchants and businesspeople. Most Vietnamese Cambodians live in rural areas in the east, near the Vietnamese border. In general, the Chinese have blended in well with the dominant Khmer population. Most have adopted Khmer customs and speak the Khmer language. The Vietnamese, on the other hand, are not so well adapted. Over the centuries, Vietnam and Cambodia have had many border conflicts and other military clashes. In modern times, the Khmers tend to treat the Vietnamese in Cambodia with distrust and hostility.

A number of smaller ethnic groups are found scattered throughout the country. The Cham, most of whom follow the Islamic (Muslim) religion, reside in small villages along the Mekong and Tonle Sap Rivers. The Khmer Loeu, or highland people, belong to a variety of different tribes, all descended from the earliest inhabitants of Southeast Asia.

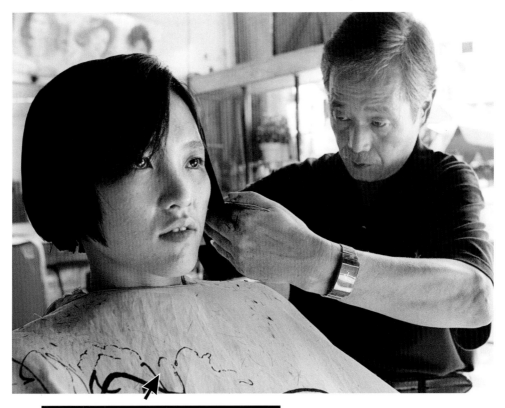

A young Chinese Cambodian gets a haircut in a beauty salon in Phnom Penh.

These groups live mainly in the isolated hills and mountains of north-eastern Cambodia. Many Khmer Loeu practice slash-and-burn agriculture, which involves cutting a section of rain forest and burning it to clear the land for farming. When the land loses its fertility, the inhabitants move on to a different area.

> To view colorful photographs, to find out more about the various customs of people in Cambodia—including various regional groups—and to get the most up-to-date population figures and other information, visit vgsbooks.com.

◉ Sanitation and Health Care

Cambodia is one of the poorest countries in Asia. The typical adult earns the equivalent of about $260 per year. According to Cambodian government figures, about 36 percent of the nation's people are classified as poor. In the countryside, only 26 percent of the population has a source of safe, clean drinking water. That figure is only 65 percent in the cities. In rural areas, most toilets are primitive, often just pits dug into the ground. In these conditions, disease is quick to spread. Malaria, dengue fever, typhus, and other illnesses are common in Cambodia.

To make matters worse, the nation's medical facilities are poorly equipped, especially in rural areas. Many doctors and nurses were killed during the Khmer Rouge regime, and a new generation of medical professionals has yet to be trained. Years of warfare have further weakened the nation's health-care system. Many rural Cambodians treat illnesses with medicinal plants and herbs—some of which are effective, others ineffective. Phnom Penh and other big cities have the nation's best health-care facilities, including hospitals and well-stocked pharmacies.

Despite some modern facilities, the combination of hunger, poor sanitation, and poor medical care creates a bleak overall health situation in Cambodia. Infant mortality (death) rates are among the highest in Southeast Asia, with 64 infant deaths for every 1,000 births. Maternal mortality (the death of a mother around the time of childbirth) is also high, with 650 deaths for every 100,000 births. Many Cambodian children are underweight and malnourished. One child in ten will die before the age of five. Diarrhea, an intestinal condition often caused by tainted food or water, is the major killer of Cambodian children.

In Cambodia good medical clinics, such as this specialized **maternity clinic** serving mothers and their children, are rare and crowded.

Cambodia has the highest rate of HIV (human immunodeficiency virus) infection in Southeast Asia. Approximately 2.8 percent of adult Cambodians are infected with HIV, the virus that causes acquired immunodeficiency syndrome (AIDS). AIDS has already killed 80,000 Cambodians, and that figure is expected to rise to 230,000 by 2010. Thousands of Cambodian children have been orphaned by the disease.

In recent years, Cambodia has taken steps to reduce its HIV/AIDS rate. Working with international health organizations, the Cambodian government has developed programs to educate people about HIV/AIDS prevention. The programs promote the use of condoms, which help prevent the sexual spread of HIV. HIV rates have decreased in Cambodia in the early 2000s, especially among prostitutes. But the virus is still widespread and remains a serious threat to the nation's future.

A Cambodian social worker displays an **AIDS prevention poster** written in the Khmer language.

Drug use poses another serious threat to Cambodian society. Many Cambodian young people use heroin and other dangerous drugs, especially in urban areas. Not only are such drugs harmful in and of themselves, but intravenous drug use (shooting drugs with needles) is also linked to HIV infection. In May 2003, the Cambodian government held a national workshop to discuss drug use in the country and ways to fight the problem.

Education

During his first reign, King Norodom Sihanouk was a great champion of education. In the 1950s and 1960s, he built hundreds of schools and universities across the country. By the 1970s, more than 2 million Cambodian children were enrolled in school.

But education came to a halt with the Khmer Rouge, which shut down all the nation's schools and executed many teachers, university students, and other scholars. As a result, most people who grew up during the Khmer Rouge period are illiterate, unable to read and write. When the PRK government came to power in Cambodia, it reopened and repaired schools and universities. Rebuilding the school system was difficult, however. Teachers, books, and equipment were all in short supply. The government had very little money to pay for school systems.

The 1993 constitution states that Cambodia will provide public education for all the nation's children, and the government has worked hard to put an educational system into place. By 1997 more than 78 percent of school-age children were enrolled in school. By 1999 the nation had more than 5,000 primary schools, 350 secondary, or middle schools, and 125 high schools. It had more than 60,000 trained teachers and nearly 2.5 million students. By 2002, 65 percent of all Cambodians were literate.

Teacher-training schools, such as this one in Kampong Cham, rushed to educate new teachers after the Khmer Rouge lost power.

Not all Cambodians receive the same amount of education, however. For instance, boys usually attend school longer than girls. Although roughly equal numbers of boys and girls attend primary school, by high school, only about one-third of the students are girls. As a result, literacy figures are much higher for Cambodian men than for women. Rural children also receive less schooling than urban children. Some rural children may not have a school nearby. Others do not attend school because their labor is needed at home, where they spend their days doing farmwork with their parents.

Many Cambodian boys study at wats, where they receive a religious as well as an academic education (girls are not allowed to study at wats). Eight colleges and universities also operate in Cambodia, with about 35,000 students enrolled. There are special colleges devoted to music, dance, and fine arts.

Some Cambodian children, such as these **students** in Kandal Province *(right)* go to school. But because of family poverty, more than **300,000 children must work.**

CULTURAL LIFE

With its ancient roots and rich history, Cambodia also has a rich cultural life. The splendid structures at Angkor are the most visible symbols of its cultural wealth, but the nation also has a strong tradition of dance, music, crafts, and storytelling. King Sihanouk was an enthusiastic patron of the arts. During his first reign, the government established a national school of music, a national school of ballet and theater, and a fine arts university.

Cambodia also has a complex religious heritage, encompassing Buddhism, Hinduism, and other ancient faiths. Wats have long been centers of Cambodian art and learning. Much of everyday life in Cambodia revolves around religious tradition and worship.

Cultural life was thoroughly suppressed during the Khmer Rouge regime. Most artists, musicians, dancers, and writers were killed. Many books, statues, and musical instruments were destroyed. Thousands of wats were also destroyed, and most of the nation's Buddhist monks were murdered. Yet the Khmer Rouge did not

destroy the temples at Angkor, although they were neglected during this era.

With Cambodia's return to normalcy in recent years, the nation's arts are once again flourishing. Wats have been rebuilt, and Cambodians are again free to pursue spiritual, cultural, and recreational activities. Arts organizations have been restored or newly formed, and new performance venues have opened. While much of Cambodian art and culture is rooted in centuries-old tradition, Cambodians have also started to embrace modern media, art, and music.

Religion

The Cambodian constitution guarantees freedom of religion for all citizens, but Buddhism is the official religion of Cambodia. About 95 percent of Cambodians are Buddhists, with the remaining 5 percent practicing Hinduism, Islam, Christianity, and animist, or traditional, religions.

Buddhism traces its origins to Siddhartha Gautama, an Indian prince who lived around 500 B.C. Weary of his privileged life, Gautama embraced spirituality and practiced fasting and meditation. He believed that through right actions and thought, a person could overcome desire, which he saw as the root of the world's suffering. He described an eightfold path to reach nirvana—a state of being without desire or suffering. After reaching nirvana, Gautama took the name Buddha, meaning "enlightened one." Indian traders and settlers brought Buddhism to Cambodia in the early years of the Funan Kingdom. Eventually, Buddhism spread to become the nation's dominant religion.

Most Cambodians practice Theravada Buddhism, one of the two main branches of Buddhism. Theravada Buddhism limits its doctrines to the teachings of the Buddha. The other main branch, Mahayana Buddhism (practiced in China and elsewhere), includes the writings and lessons of other teachers and promotes a belief in many Buddhas. Many Chinese Cambodians follow Mahayana Buddhism.

Buddhism in Cambodia centers on the village wat, where Buddhist monks—male religious teachers—live and worship. The monks play a vital role in Cambodian communities. For instance, monks participate in all religious festivals as well as weddings, funerals, and other ceremonies. In the morning, monks leave the temple and walk along the street, accepting offerings of food from the villagers. They typically wear orange robes and have close-shaved heads.

A reclining Buddha statue dominates this shrine at Wat Lang Ka in Phnom Penh.

Buddhist monks

Every male Buddhist is expected to become a monk for at least a short time after he finishes school and before he marries. The usual time served is about three months, but some men choose to remain monks for part or all of their adult lives. Women may become Buddhist nuns, which some do, especially in middle age. Nuns carry out specific tasks at wats, such as preparing altars (platforms where religious rituals take place) or housekeeping. Many nuns are widows.

Traders also brought Hinduism, another ancient Indian religion, to Cambodia in the early years of Funan. Until the fourteenth century, Hinduism was widespread in Cambodia. The magnificent temple of Angkor Wat, created in the twelfth century A.D., was built to honor the Hindu god Vishnu. Gradually, more and more Cambodians adopted Theravada Buddhism, and Hinduism began to decline. In modern times, Hindus make up a very small portion of the Cambodian population.

The Cham, an ethnic group whose ancestors came from the ancient kingdom of Champa, are Muslims. Muslims practice Islam, a religion founded in the Middle East in the seventh century A.D. by the prophet Muhammad. Many immigrants from Malaysia to Cambodia also practice Islam. During the late 1970s, the Khmer Rouge killed many Muslims and destroyed mosques, or Islamic houses of worship. Many mosques have since been rebuilt.

The French introduced Christianity into Southeast Asia during the colonial era. But few Cambodians adopted the religion, and it remains very limited in Cambodia. The Khmer Rouge destroyed many Christian churches during its reign.

A **Muslim Cambodian boy** heads home from his school, located at a rural mosque.

The Khmer Loeu peoples of northeastern Cambodia hold animist beliefs. Animism involves worshipping the spirits of natural objects such as rocks and trees, as well as the spirits of one's ancestors. Cambodians practiced animism long before Buddhism and Hinduism arrived from India. Over the years, as these religions spread through Cambodia, they also fused with traditional animist beliefs. As a result, Cambodian Buddhists also follow some animist practices, such as ancestor worship.

Language and Literature

Cambodia's official language is Khmer, which has its roots in the ancient languages of southern India. The oldest Khmer inscriptions (writings in stone) date to the seventh century A.D.

The Khmer alphabet has fifty-seven letters (compared to just twenty-six letters in English). These letters look nothing like the alphabet used to write English and other European languages. For non-Cambodians, Khmer can be difficult to learn and pronounce. However, Khmer grammar (rules about language structure) is very simple. Khmer is spoken throughout the country, although several regions have local dialects, or variations on the main language.

The French language arrived in the 1800s with French soldiers and government officials. From the late 1800s to the 1960s, French was Cambodia's second most common language. Most older Cambodians studied French at school and still speak it, and many French words have made their way into Khmer. But French is less prevalent than it used to be in Cambodia. English has become increasingly common, especially as more and more tourists arrive from English-speaking countries and as Cambodians engage in more international business. Modern Cambodian students learn both Khmer and English at school. Malay, Vietnamese, and Cantonese (a Chinese dialect) are commonly heard in Phnom Penh.

Cambodian literature has been passed down from generation to generation. This literature includes stories about the Buddha, poems that offer advice about day-to-day life, epic (extremely long) tales originating in ancient India, and a variety of folktales, songs,

SOME KHMER TERMS AND THEIR MEANINGS

KHMER	ENGLISH
Angkor	royal city
phnom	mountain
stung	river
tonle	large river
wat	temple

To learn more about the Khmer language and other aspects of Cambodian culture, visit vgsbooks.com for links.

and legends. Centuries ago, some of these works were written on palm leaves, but these leaves have, of course, decayed. Even without written copies, the literature was well preserved by storytellers and traveling minstrels, who performed the works at festivals and on village streets. Some storytellers memorized epic works that took many days to recite. The French brought printing technology to Cambodia, and the old stories were then transferred to books. Some of them were later made into films, television shows, and even comic strips.

> **Don't let an angry man wash dishes. Don't let a hungry man guard rice.**
>
> —Cambodian proverbs

In the 1930s, Cambodians began to write new literature, including novels. The nation's publishing industry prospered until the Khmer Rouge took over. Then, books and library buildings were destroyed, and writers were killed. New literature was banned, except for songs, poems, and texts that praised the Khmer Rouge and its revolutionary ideas.

With the Khmer Rouge gone, Cambodians have begun to revive their literary traditions. Classic works have been reprinted, libraries have been rebuilt, and a new generation is learning about ancient Cambodian tales and poems. More new novels have been written too. A number of contemporary writers, including Chanrithy Him and Loung Ung, have written memoirs about the horrors of the Khmer Rouge regime and their struggles to survive in that era.

Modern Media

Modern modes of communication (telephones, computers, and Internet service) are available in Cambodia, but the nation lags far behind Western countries in high technology. In the early twenty-first century, about 110,000 Cambodians (less than 1 percent of the people) had cellular or home telephones. Only 15,000 had personal computers, and only 6,000 had Internet access. Most telecommunications users and providers are located in Phnom Penh and other big cities. Many rural areas have no phone or electrical service at all.

More than ten radio stations and five television stations broadcast in Cambodia. Some stations are run by the government. Several stations broadcast in English and French. The nation has more than twenty newspapers, some written in Khmer, some in English, some in French. It also has a small film industry. A few Cambodian-made films, such as Rithy Panh's *One Evening after the War* (1998), have examined post–Khmer Rouge Cambodia.

◉ Architecture, Arts, and Crafts

Cambodia's principal works of art and architecture are found at the temple complex of Angkor. Over a period of five hundred years—between the ninth and fourteenth centuries—skilled artists, craftspeople, and laborers created Angkor's sculptures, temples, and other structures. Although the buildings and artwork have suffered damage from centuries of heat, monsoon rains, neglect, and war, Angkor remains a splendid monument to the Khmer Empire. It is the largest religious shrine in Southeast Asia.

Once a thriving capital city, Angkor contains approximately one hundred sandstone and brick temples. The city was also once filled with wooden houses, government buildings, and palaces, but these structures decayed long ago. The temples that remain were built by Khmer kings as monuments to their own greatness and achievements, as well as to honor their gods. The kings were also buried inside their temples. Most Khmer kings were Hindus, and their temples feature images of Hindu gods. King Jayavarman VII, the last ruler to build temples at Angkor, was a Buddhist. The structures built during his reign contain many Buddhist images.

In addition to the temples, the complex includes magnificent terraces, gates, statues, pools, and other monuments. The structures are adorned with carvings of gods, goddesses, angels, devils, armies, animals, and mythological beasts. The largest, best-preserved, and most famous temple is Angkor Wat, built during the reign of Suryavarman II (1112–1152). This massive temple contains countless splendors, including a giant statue of the eight-armed Hindu god Vishnu.

Ancient craftspeople also created smaller artworks such as handwoven silk; stone sculptures; wooden carvings of the Buddha, animals, and other objects; exquisite silverwork; pottery; and jewelry. These craft traditions have continued into modern times. The National Museum

The giant Vishnu statue at Angkor Wat is 10 feet (3.3 m) tall.

of Cambodia in Phnom Penh displays a range of Cambodian arts dating from the early days of Funan. Although the museum was looted and damaged during the reign of the Khmer Rouge, much of its collection survived and has been restored.

Performing Arts

Dance has long been entwined with Cambodian culture. In earlier centuries, Cambodian kings kept troupes of female dancers in the royal court. Royal dances featured precise hand movements and graceful poses. Dancers wore shimmering sequined costumes and fancy headdresses. Although the Cambodian king no longer keeps royal dancers, the style continues at the Royal Ballet in Phnom Penh.

Folk dances were also common in early Cambodia. Many dances involved spirit worship. For instance, at religious ceremonies people danced to ask the gods for rain, a good harvest, or other good fortune. Other dances were based on Hindu myths, epics, and folktales. These were often performed by troupes of male dancers who toured from village to village.

Music, too, has a long tradition in Cambodia. Sculptures at Angkor show musicians playing stringed instruments, wind instruments, drums, and xylophones. Royal and folk dances were always accompanied by bands of musicians. People sang songs at work, play, weddings, and festivals. The old songs and musical styles remained popular until the 1970s, when the Khmer Rouge killed most musicians. In the modern era, new styles are emerging in Phnom Penh and other cities. These styles combine traditional Cambodian sounds with Western pop music, including rap.

Sports and Recreation

Cambodians enjoy a variety of sports and games. One popular game, *pétanque*, came to Cambodia from France. Pétanque is similar to horseshoes and lawn bowling. Players take turns tossing steel balls at a smaller wooden ball. At the end of the game, the player whose steel ball sits closest to the wooden ball is the winner. Cambodian children and teenagers play a game called *ang kunh*. In this game, teams of players throw large (egg-sized) seeds, trying to hit the seeds of their opponents. *Leak kong saeng*, or "hide the handkerchief," is another fun children's game. It's a lot like duck duck goose, but players tag one another with a knotted handkerchief. Played on chalk squares drawn on the sidewalk, *mek* is a little like hopscotch. Along with hopping from square to square, players also kick a sandal or flip-flop from one square to the next.

Canoe races are an exciting part of Cambodia's Bon Om Tuk, the three-day water festival in late October or early November. Villages build and decorate dugouts that can hold as many as forty rowers. Boats race in pairs until the last day, when all race.

Cambodians enjoy watching spectator sports, such as soccer. In 1996 Cambodia sent ten athletes to the Summer Olympic Games in Atlanta, Georgia. Because of warfare, this was the first time in twenty-four years that Cambodia had been able to participate in the games.

Festivals and Holidays

Cambodians observe a variety of holidays, some religious and some secular (nonreligious). Many holidays follow the lunar (moon-based) calendar, which changes every year. As a result, the holidays don't have fixed dates. Major holidays are

- National Day—early January: commemorates the overthrow of the Khmer Rouge
- Chaul Chnam—mid-April (three days): the Cambodian New Year
- International Workers' Day—May 1: a day to honor laborers
- Chat Preah Nengkai—early May: an agricultural festival
- Genocide Day—May 9: a day of mourning for those killed by the Khmer Rouge
- Visakha Puja—mid-May: honors Gautama Buddha's birth, enlightenment, and attainment of nirvana
- P'chum Ben—late September: a day to honor one's ancestors
- Bon Om Tuk—late October or early November: a water festival, held when the Tonle Sap River reverses course and flows back into the Mekong
- Independence Day—November 9: honors Cambodian independence from France in 1953

Food

Cambodian cuisine has a lot in common with the foods of Thailand, Vietnam, Malaysia, and China. The most common ingredients are rice, noodles, fish, and vegetables (including cabbage, carrots, cucumbers, mushrooms, and onions). Herbs such as coriander, lemongrass, and mint leaves provide flavoring in many dishes. The most popular drink is tea.

Fish—caught fresh from lakes and rivers—has always been a mainstay of the Cambodian diet. Cambodians prepare fish in several ways. It can be grilled, steamed, stuffed with dried shrimp, wrapped in lettuce or spinach leaves and dipped in sauce, or cooked with vegetables in a wok (a round steel cooking pan). Meats such as chicken, pork, and beef are more expensive than fish and so are less common in Cambodian cooking.

Like fish, rice is a staple of the Cambodian diet. The nation's most plentiful crop, rice is usually served fried. Soup is another common dish. Favorites include hot-and-sour fish soup, ginger-flavored pork soup, and shrimp soup. Soup is usually served slightly warmed or at room temperature. Another favorite is salad, which commonly includes greens, herbs, beef, and cooked egg. Cambodians also enjoy a variety of noodle dishes, including rice noodles cooked in coconut milk.

Many tropical fruits grow in Cambodia, and people enjoy fruit-filled snacks and desserts. Examples include jackfruit pudding, coconut pastries, and rice cakes with banana filling. On holidays and other special occasions, people eat balls of sticky rice mixed with fresh bananas. Some Cambodian fruits (pineapples, bananas, and mangoes) are familiar to Western visitors, while others (durians, mangosteens, and rambutans) are more exotic.

KUAY NAMUAN

Kuay namuan is a popular Cambodian dessert, which includes two common Cambodian fruits: bananas and coconuts.

2 tablespoons sugar

2 cups coconut milk

8 large ripe bananas, cut into 3 or 4 pieces each

1. In a medium saucepan, mix sugar and coconut milk and simmer on the stove until thick and creamy.
2. Add bananas and cook gently until soft but not mushy.
3. Serve warm.

Serves 6

THE ECONOMY

Cambodia's economy has long been based on agriculture. Rural families traditionally produced the food they needed to survive, mainly by growing rice and other crops and by fishing in lakes and rivers. The French opened rubber plantations in Cambodia during colonial times. Through much of the twentieth century, rice and rubber were Cambodia's principal moneymakers. Tourism also contributed to the nation's income, as did industries such as paper-making, food processing, and textile manufacturing.

When war came—first the U.S. bombing and then the Khmer Rouge takeover—the Cambodian economy utterly collapsed. Roads, farms, and factories were destroyed. What's more, in their drive to remake Cambodia into a Communist farming society, the Khmer Rouge abolished money, blew up banks, shut down stores, and cut off business with most of the outside world. The Khmer Rouge killed many people and worked others nearly to death. Disease and starvation spread throughout the country.

Even after the Vietnamese took over from the Khmer Rouge, the nation still suffered from famine, guerrilla warfare, and economic despair. International agencies shipped food to the starving people, but soldiers stole many of the food shipments. For most of the 1980s, the nation was gripped by poverty.

The arrival of the United Nations Transitional Authority in Cambodia (UNTAC) in 1991 proved to be an important turning point. The thousands of foreign troops and administrators who came to oversee the creation of a new democratic government in Cambodia needed food, housing, and consumer goods. The country began stocking up to supply the UN workers. New stores were opened. New buildings were constructed. As a result, Cambodia's gross domestic product (GDP)—the total value of all goods and services produced within the country in a year—rose by 13.5 percent in 1991 and by 8 percent the following year. In addition, Japan, France, the United States, and other nations sent about $1 billion in aid to help the new government, with additional funds provided by the World Bank and the International Monetary Fund.

Throughout the 1990s, the economy continued to recover and grow. In 1999 Cambodia was admitted to the Association of Southeast Asian Nations (ASEAN), an organization that works to improve economic, cultural, and social welfare in Southeast Asia. New industries opened, and tourism increased, making the country less reliant on agriculture for its economic well-being. Although Cambodia still relies on foreign aid and many people are poor, there is great optimism for the future. Most important, Cambodia has been relatively peaceful for more than a decade. Many people are hopeful that peace will lead to prosperity.

Agriculture

The agricultural sector (farming, fishing, and forestry) is Cambodia's major industry, accounting for 50 percent of the nation's gross domestic product. About 80 percent of Cambodians make their living in this sector. Most farms are located in the central basin around the Tonle Sap Lake and the Mekong River. In general, Cambodian farms are small, family-owned enterprises.

Rice is the nation's primary crop, but some farmers grow potatoes, yams, soybeans, mung beans, sesame seeds, peanuts, corn, cucumbers, and peppers. Others grow fruits such as bananas, coconuts, mangoes, papayas, and pineapples. Some farmers raise poultry and hogs. Many make their living by fishing. The Tonle Sap Lake and River, the Mekong, and other rivers provide abundant catches of perch, lungfish, eels, carps, and smelts. Some farmers practice aquaculture—a system of raising fish in artificial ponds. Fishing accounts for about 3.5 percent of Cambodia's GDP.

Despite improvements in the economy, large numbers of Cambodians are very poor. Approximately 75 percent of Cambodian workers are subsistence farmers. That is, the farmers produce only enough food to feed themselves and their families, without any left over to sell.

The rice business accounts for 15 percent of Cambodia's GDP. Rice is grown in paddies, or flooded fields. Most Cambodian farmers are very poor and cannot afford mechanized equipment. Many work the fields with hand tools and use oxen or water buffalo to pull plows. The rice crop is always vulnerable to drought, flooding (floods in 2001 damaged about 15 percent of the nation's rice fields), and drops in world rice prices. A poor rice harvest can damage the nation's economy and even cause famine. On the positive side, the Cambodian government and international organizations have recently begun programs to modernize Cambodian rice farms. New varieties of rice, better fertilizers, pest management systems, and new equipment promise to lead to higher crop yields and a stronger overall economy.

Natural rubber, used to make tires, elastic bands, and other products, comes from latex, the milky white juice of the rubber tree. Rubber trees grow well in tropical countries. Grown on plantations, natural rubber was once one of Cambodia's most important agricultural products, second only to rice. Cambodia's rubber industry is no longer as strong as it used to be, however. Firstly, many rubber plantations were abandoned or destroyed during the Khmer Rouge era. Secondly, with the rise of the synthetic rubber industry (synthetic rubber is made from chemicals), the natural rubber industry has declined worldwide. Nevertheless, rubber production is still an important industry in Cambodia, and plans are under way to revitalize the sector. Most of Cambodia's rubber is exported, either as raw latex or as finished tires for vehicles.

Cambodia's rain forests are among the nation's most valuable natural resources and among the most threatened. Throughout the late 1900s, the forests were cut at an alarming rate. Six provinces have been nearly cleared of wood, and less than half of the nation's original rain forests remain. The Cambodian government puts few restrictions on logging companies, and many loggers operate illegally. The future of the logging industry presents a dilemma for Cambodia. On the one hand, timber sales bring much-needed income to the country. Logging accounted for almost half the country's export earnings in the 1990s. The nation also profits from

Selling firewood

related industries, such as wood processing, paper production, and printing. On the other hand, aggressive logging has led to environmental destruction such as erosion, flooding, and the destruction of wildlife habitat.

◉ Industry

Cambodia's industrial sector encompasses mining, processing raw materials, and manufacturing. This sector is growing quickly. In the early twenty-first century, industry accounted for 15 percent of Cambodia's GDP. In the past, the government owned and controlled most manufacturing operations. Many state-owned facilities proved to be inefficient, however. In the early 1990s, the Cambodian government began privatizing many businesses—that is, selling them to private companies. Many foreign and domestic investors have bought and modernized previously state-run enterprises.

By 2001 more than 300 factories were operating in Cambodia, employing roughly 215,000 Cambodians. Most of the factories (75 percent) manufacture garments, including well-known Western brands such as Calvin Klein and Gap. Other factories produce or process food, wood products, tobacco, beverages, nails, automobile and bicycle tires, tools, and medicines.

Cambodia has mineral and energy resources, but these are just newly being mined. Mineral deposits include iron ore, limestone, kaolin, silver, and gold. Offshore oil and gas reserves have been located in the Gulf of Thailand, and drilling has begun there. Hydroelectric dams promise to provide much-needed electrical power throughout the country. Dams have already been built on several small rivers, with some planned for the Mekong.

The Service Sector

The service sector, including tourism, banking, transportation, and communications, accounts for 35 percent of Cambodia's GDP. By far the most important industry is tourism (unheard of during the war years), with the number of foreign tourists growing about 30 percent a year in the late 1990s. In 2000 more than 350,000 visitors came to Cambodia, many from the United States and Europe. Most tourists want to visit Angkor Wat, but they also explore the nation's beaches, parks, and cities. The tourists have money to spend, and thousands of Cambodians have been newly employed in the tourism industry.

To accommodate the tourists, the nation has built dozens of new hotels and restaurants. Roads have been improved, and the airport at Phnom Penh has been renovated. The government has also made it

The Grand Hotel of Angkor in Siem Reap offers tourists many comforts.

A man crafts a new statue at a Buddha factory in Phnom Penh. **These tourists,** are visiting Banteay Srei, a tenth-century temple 15 miles (24 km) from Angkor. Discover Cambodian tourist spots at vgsbooks.com.

easier for travelers to get visas—documents that allow foreigners to visit the country. The majority of tourists fly into Cambodia from Bangkok, Thailand.

Cambodia is by no means high tech when it comes to transportation. Most roads are unpaved and have been damaged by war, weather, and neglect. However, a major road rebuilding program is under way, with funding from international aid agencies. In total, the nation has 22,000 miles of highways, less than 10 percent of them paved, and 375 miles of railroad track. Buses run between most cities and villages. Ferryboats take people across the Mekong River. Phnom Penh, on the Mekong, and Sihanoukville, on the Gulf of Thailand, are the nation's major water ports. The nation also has twenty airports, but only five of them have paved runways. Phnom Penh has the most modern airport, with regular flights to Thailand, Hong Kong, Malaysia, Singapore, and Laos.

The Future

Cambodia is experiencing a rebirth. The atrocities of the Khmer Rouge regime are fading into history. A new generation of Cambodians is growing up in a free and democratic society. Many obstacles remain, however, including a high HIV/AIDS rate, dangerous landmines, poor health care, and high rates of poverty. These problems are very real and are not likely to be solved easily. But with international assistance, a stable government, a lasting peace, and a growing economy, Cambodia may at last be on the path toward prosperity.

Timeline

PRE-4000 B.C. People migrate to Cambodia from neighboring regions.

CA. 200 B.C. Khmer peoples move to Cambodia from southern China.

A.D. 0-100 The kingdom of Funan, based in Cambodia, grows in Southeast Asia.

600s The state of Chenla takes over Funan.

802 King Jayavarman II begins to unify the Khmers into a single state.

LATE 900s Khmer kings begin to build monuments at Angkor.

EARLY 1100s King Suryavarman II builds Angkor Wat, a temple complex honoring the Hindu god Vishnu.

1181 Jayavarman VII, a Buddhist, becomes king. Buddhism grows more dominant in Cambodia.

1430s The Khmer abandon Angkor and establish a new capital at Phnom Penh.

1431 Thai armies sack Angkor for the second time.

1500s Merchants from China, the Middle East, and Europe begin to trade heavily in Southeast Asia, including Cambodia.

CA. 1620 The Khmer make an alliance with the Vietnamese, allowing Vietnamese people to settle in the Mekong River delta.

1772 Thai forces burn Phnom Penh to the ground.

LATE 1700s Thailand and Vietnam take control of the Cambodian government.

EARLY 1800s France tries to expand its territory and control in Southeast Asia.

1860s Henri Mouhot, a French naturalist, publishes a book about Angkor, creating worldwide interest in the ancient city.

1863 Cambodia signs a treaty with the French, giving France access to Cambodia's natural resources in exchange for military protection.

1884 Cambodia becomes a French colony.

EARLY 1900s French colonists establish new roads, railroads, and plantations in Cambodia.

1927 Cambodian peasants rebel unsuccessfully against French-run labor and taxation systems.

1941-1945 Japan occupies Cambodia and other Southeast Asian nations during World War II. The Japanese let France continue to run the Cambodian government, however.

1945	World War II ends, and France returns to power in Cambodia.
1946	France allows Cambodians to elect a national assembly and write a constitution.
1953	Cambodia gains its independence from France.
1957	North Vietnamese guerrillas attack South Vietnam.
1965	Norodom Sihanouk, then Cambodia's prime minister, lets North Vietnamese and Vietnamese Communists (Viet Cong) station troops in Cambodia.
1969	The United States begins bombing eastern Cambodia.
1970	General Lon Nol overthrows Sihanouk's government.
Early 1970s	The Khmer Rouge canvasses the Cambodian countryside, gaining support for its Communist movement.
1975	Led by Pol Pot, the Khmer Rouge takes over Phnom Penh and evacuates the city. It begins a reign of terror marked by brutality, torture, and mass killings.
1978–1979	Vietnam invades Cambodia and sets up a new government.
1979	Famine strikes Cambodia. Hundreds of thousands flee to refugee camps in Thailand.
1991	Vietnam gives up control of Cambodia.
1992	Angkor becomes a UNESCO world heritage site.
1993	The United Nations oversees elections for a new Cambodian national assembly. The assembly creates a new national constitution.
Mid-1990s	More than 350,000 refugees return from Thailand. The Khmer Rouge continues to operate in the Cambodian countryside.
1998	Cambodia holds new elections for the national assembly. Hun Sen becomes sole prime minister. Pol Pot dies.
1999	Cambodia becomes a member of ASEAN, an association of Southeast Asian states.
2000	Tourism swells in Cambodia, with more than 350,000 visitors in one year.
2003	The United Nations approves a plan for war crimes trials against former Khmer Rouge leaders.

COUNTRY NAME Kingdom of Cambodia

AREA 69,898 square miles (181,000 sq. km)

MAIN LANDFORMS Tonle Sap basin; Mekong River valley; Dangrek, Elephant, Cardamom Mountains; Central Cambodian Plain

HIGHEST POINT Mount Aôral, 5,947 feet (1,813 m) above sea level

LOWEST POINT Sea level

MAJOR RIVERS Mekong, Tonle Sap, Bassac, Sangker

ANIMALS Tigers, bears, panthers, wild oxen, deer, monkeys, elephants, herons, cranes, pelicans, cormorants, egrets, ducks, grouse, pheasants, peacocks, snakes, geckos, catfish, carp, lungfish, perch, smelts, frogs, prawns, turtles

CAPITAL CITY Phnom Penh

OTHER MAJOR CITIES Sihanoukville, Battambang, Siem Reap

OFFICIAL LANGUAGE Khmer

MONETARY UNIT Riel. 1 riel = 100 sen

CAMBODIAN CURRENCY

During the Khmer Rouge era, Cambodia had no currency, because the Khmer Rouge abolished money and even blew up banks. After the Khmer Rouge lost power, Cambodians returned to using their standard unit of currency, called the riel. One riel is not worth very much money. In fact, it takes almost 4,000 riel to equal just one U.S. dollar. The Cambodian government issues 100, 200, 500, 1,000, 2,000, 5,000, 10,000, 20,000, 50,000, and 100,000 riel notes (paper money). Cambodians also make transactions using U.S. dollars and Thai currency, called baht.

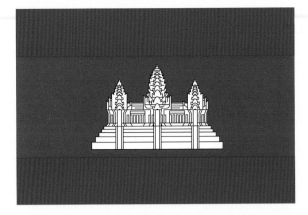

The Cambodian flag has three horizontal stripes: blue on top and bottom and red in the middle. The Angkor Wat temple is pictured in white inside the red stripe. The first Cambodian flag was designed during the French colonial era. The flag was redesigned several times over the years, depending on who controlled the country. The modern flag is based on a design used from 1948 to 1970.

The Cambodian national anthem, "Nokoreach," was written by a man named Chuon Nat. Its name comes from an ancient Khmer kingdom. Its tune comes from an old Cambodian folk song. The anthem was adopted in 1941, but the Khmer Rouge replaced it with a new anthem in 1975. When Cambodia wrote its new constitution in 1993, it restored "Nokoreach" as its national anthem. The original anthem was sung in Khmer and sometimes French. Here is the English translation:

Heaven protects our King
And gives him happiness and glory
To reign over our souls and our destinies,
The one being, heir of the Sovereign builders,
Guiding the proud old Kingdom.

Temples are asleep in the forest,
Remembering the splendor of Moha Nokor.
Like a rock the Khmer race is eternal.
Let us trust in the fate of Kampuchea,
The empire which challenges the ages.

Songs rise up from the pagodas
To the glory of holy Buddhistic faith.
Let us be faithful to our ancestors' belief.
Thus heaven will lavish its bounty
Toward the ancient Khmer country, the Moha Nokor.

For a link where you can listen to Cambodia's national anthem, "Nokoreach," go to vgsbooks.com.

CHANRITHY HIM (b. 1965) Writer Chanrithy Him was born in Phnom Penh Province, and she was ten years old when the Khmer Rouge took power in Cambodia. She and her family endured disease and starvation in the forced labor camps and witnessed tortures and executions. From a family of twelve, only five Him children survived the ordeal. After the Khmer Rouge lost power, the surviving children were able to migrate to Oregon (with the help of an uncle who was already in the United States). Him lives in Eugene, Oregon, where she works with the Khmer Adolescent Project, a group that studies post-traumatic stress disorder among Khmer Rouge–era survivors. Her 2000 memoir, *When Broken Glass Floats*, recounts her terrifying childhood experiences.

HAING NGOR (1950–1996) Born in Samrong Young and trained as a physician, Ngor became a captive of the Khmer Rouge in the late 1970s. Hiding his identity as an educated professional, he managed to escape execution. Along with his orphaned niece, he fled to a refugee camp in Thailand and then immigrated to the United States. Although he had no prior acting experience, he was chosen to play photographer Dith Pran in *The Killing Fields*, an acclaimed 1984 film about the Khmer Rouge era. Ngor won an Academy Award as Best Supporting Actor for his role in the film. He went on to appear in several additional films. He wrote his autobiography, *Haing Ngor: A Cambodian Odyssey*, in 1988. The target of a robbery attempt in Los Angeles in 1996, Ngor was shot and killed.

RITHY PANH (b. 1964) Born in Phnom Penh, Panh endured the Khmer Rouge camps before escaping to Thailand in 1979. A year later, he moved to Paris, where he studied filmmaking. His films include *Site 2* (1989), a documentary about Cambodian refugees; *People of the Rice Fields* (1995), which examines Cambodian peasant life; and *One Evening after the War* (1998), about postwar Phnom Penh. Panh has won numerous awards for his work.

DITH PRAN (b. 1942) Angkor Wat–born Dith Pran worked as a war correspondent in Cambodia during the Vietnam War/Khmer Rouge era. His horrific experiences at the hands of the Khmer Rouge are portrayed in *The Killing Fields*, a 1984 drama. Pran later moved to the United States, where he works as a photojournalist, lecturer, and activist. He is founder and president of the Dith Pran Holocaust Awareness Project, a group that works to educate people about the crimes of the Khmer Rouge. He also compiled *Children of Cambodia's Killing Fields: Memoirs by Survivors* (1997).

SOPHILINE CHEAM SHAPIRO (b. 1967) Sophiline Cheam was born in Phnom Penh and endured the brutal Khmer Rouge regime as a child. When the country returned to peace, she entered Phnom Penh's Ecole de Beaux Arts (School of Fine Arts), where she studied classical Cambodian court dance. She graduated in 1988 and then joined the school's dance faculty. In addition to teaching, she toured nationally and internationally with the Classical Dance Company of Cambodia. She married an American, John Shapiro, and moved with him to Los Angeles in 1991. She continued teaching and performing and also earned a bachelor's degree from the University of California in 1997. Shapiro is a leader in California's large Cambodian community, working with many arts, health-care, and educational organizations.

NORODOM SIHANOUK (b. 1922) Norodom Sihanouk, Cambodia's king, was born in Phnom Penh. He is one of the most famous names in Cambodian politics. The grandson of King Norodom, he took the throne in 1941, at only nineteen years of age. French colonial officials thought the young king would be easy to control, but he soon proved to be defiant. He led Cambodia's crusade for independence, then gave up his throne to become the country's prime minister. After his government was overthrown in 1970, Sihanouk went into exile in China. He was also imprisoned for a time by the Khmer Rouge. He returned to Cambodia in the early 1990s, once again entering politics. When a new government was formed in 1993, Sihanouk was again named king. In addition to his political activities, he has written, directed, and produced several feature-length films. Sihanoukville, on the Gulf of Thailand, is named for him.

SIN SISAMUTH (1932–1975) Called "the King of Khmer Song," Sin Sisamuth got his start singing in a restaurant in Kbal Thnol and came to fame in the 1950s. The popular songwriter and performer was known for his beautiful voice. Like thousands of other Cambodian artists, Sisamuth was executed in the first few days of the Khmer Rouge regime. Modern listeners can still enjoy his voice on recordings, and his grandson Sin Sothakol follows in his footsteps, pursuing a career as a singer.

LOUNG UNG (b. 1970) Phnom Penh–born Ung endured the Khmer Rouge era as a child. She eventually escaped to a Thai refugee camp and then moved to the United States. In the mid-1990s, she became the spokesperson for the Campaign for a Landmine Free World, operated by the Vietnam Veterans of America Foundation. In this position, she travels around the world, educating people about the dangers of landmines and working to assist landmine victims. Her book, *First They Killed My Father*, tells of her childhood experiences under the Khmer Rouge.

ANGKOR The famous Angkor complex is known worldwide for its magnificent temples, sculptures, gates, pools, and other monuments. The most famous temple is Angkor Wat, built to honor the Hindu god Vishnu. Another highlight is Angkor Thom, a fortified city built by King Jayavarman VII. Altogether, Angkor contains about one hundred temples, built over more than six hundred years of Khmer history.

BOU SRAA WATERFALL This two-tiered waterfall, located east of the city of Senmonorom, offers a spectacular display. The upper tier drops more than 30 feet (9 m), and the lower tier falls more than 80 feet (24 m). The falls are among the nation's largest.

NATIONAL MUSEUM OF CAMBODIA This museum in Phnom Penh houses treasures of Cambodia's past, including statues of Vishnu and other Hindu gods, statues of early Khmer leaders, ancient pottery and bronze work, and other art and artifacts. The museum is housed in a beautiful building with a wonderfully ornate roof.

PRASAT PREAH VIHEAR This temple, dedicated to Shiva (one of the major Hindu gods), perches atop a cliff in the Dangrek Mountains in northern Cambodia. The temple was built over a period of two hundred years, created by seven successive Khmer kings. The temple includes many exquisite carvings. The view from the top is breathtaking.

PREK TOAL BIRD SANCTUARY AND THE FLOATING VILLAGE Set on the banks of the Tonle Sap Lake, the sanctuary is home to many rare birds, including storks and pelicans. Nearby is the "floating village" of Cong Kneas. Its residents live on fishing boats. As the lake grows or shrinks with the changing seasons, the whole village moves to a new location.

THE ROYAL PALACE Built in 1866, the Royal Palace in Phnom Penh is still home to the Cambodian king and queen. The palace compound contains many impressive attractions, including the grand Throne Hall and elaborate shrines and pavilions. The highlight of the palace is the Silver Pagoda. Its floor is covered with more than five thousand silver tiles. The pagoda also contains gold, crystal, marble Buddhas, and ancient jewel-covered Khmer masks.

SIHANOUKVILLE Located on the Gulf of Thailand, Sihanoukville is a lively resort town with many restaurants, shops, and guesthouses. Visitors can swim at the city's beautiful white sand beaches and explore nearby parks, waterfalls, and islands.

TUOL SLENG MUSEUM This Phnom Penh museum documents the atrocities of the Khmer Roughe regime using photographs, artifacts, and other exhibits. Many exhibits are disturbing and painful to view.

animism: a religious practice of spirit worship. Spirits are believed to inhabit natural objects, natural events (such as storms and lightning), and human ancestors.

aquaculture: the farming of fish and other water animals, often in artificial ponds

artifact: a human-made object that remains from a particular historical period

colony: a territory governed by a distant nation and inhabited in part by settlers from that nation

Communism: a system in which the government controls the nation's economy, with no private property

delta: the triangular-shaped region of soil deposits at the mouth of a river

genocide: the deliberate and systematic killing of a racial, political, or cultural group

gross domestic product (GDP): the value of the goods and services produced by a country over a period of time, such as a year

guerrillas: small groups of fighters who operate independently, using nontraditional military practices

hydroelectric power: electricity produced by the power of rushing water. People often dam rivers to create hydroelectric power stations.

irrigation: a system of moving water to agricultural fields using canals, pipes, reservoirs, and other devices

literacy: the ability to read and write

migration: the movement of people or animals from one home to another

monsoon: a seasonal wind accompanied by heavy rainfall

parliamentary monarchy: a government that is run by both a king and an elected parliament, or legislature

rain forest: a forest growing in an area of year-round warmth and abundant rainfall

refugee: a person who flees his or her home to escape danger or persecution

subsistence farming: growing only enough food to feed one's family, without any left over to sell

tribute: payment made by one nation or person to another, often as a sign of submission

tropical region: an area close to the equatorwith heavy rainfall, high temperatures, and year-round plant growth

Selected Bibliography

"Background Note: Cambodia." *U.S. Department of State.* 1996.
Website: <http://www.state.gov/r/pa/ei/bgn/2732.htm> **(October 1, 2003).**
This Web page offers a variety of statistics and information on Cambodia, including its people, history, and government.

Central Intelligence Agency (CIA). "Cambodia." *The World Factbook,* **2002.**
Website: <http://www.cia.gov/cia/publications/factbook/geos/cb.html> **(October 1, 2003).**
The World Factbook provides basic information and statistics on Cambodia's geography, people, government, economy, communications, transportation, military, and transnational issues.

"Country Profile: Cambodia." *BBC News World Edition.* **March 11, 2003.**
Website: <http://news.bbc.co.uk/2/hi/asia-pacific/country_profiles/1243892.stm> **(October 1, 2003).**
The page offers a brief profile of Cambodia, including information on its prime minister, Hun Sen.

"Kingdom of Cambodia." *Royal Cambodian Embassy in Washington, D.C.* **2003.**
Website: <http://www.embassy.org/cambodia/> **(October 1, 2003).**
The Cambodian embassy website offers a variety of information about the nation, with links to government and tourist information.

Mazzeo, Donatella, and Chiara Silvi Antonini. *Monuments of Civilization: Ancient Cambodia.* **New York: Grosset & Dunlap, 1978.**
Illustrated with beautiful photographs, this book examines the great ancient civilizations of Cambodia, including Funan and the Khmer Empire. The book includes extensive coverage of the monuments at Angkor Wat.

Osborne, Milton. *The Mekong: Turbulent Past, Uncertain Future.* **New York: Atlantic Monthly Press, 2000.**
Osborne examines the Mekong River, which runs though Cambodia and several other Southeast Asian countries. He looks at the history of the Mekong region and issues facing the river and those who live along its banks.

Raise the Bamboo Curtain: Viet Nam, Cambodia and Burma, **dir. Rick Ray, 95 min., Wish You Were Here Productions, 1995, videocassette.**
This travel-oriented video examines modern-day Vietnam, Cambodia, and Myanmar. The Cambodian section focuses on the splendors of Angkor and the atrocities of the Khmer Rouge regime.

Ray, Nick. *Cambodia.* **Footscray, Victoria, Australia: Lonely Planet Publications, 2002.**
This guide for travelers offers exhaustive information about Cambodia, with sections on history, economy, geography, customs, tourist sites, and advice for travelers.

The Statesman's Yearbook: The Politics, Cultures, and Economies of the World 2002. New York: Palgrave Publishers Ltd., 2001.
This source presents a variety of statistics on Cambodian society, government, industry, communications, and culture. It also includes a discussion of key historical events.

Ung, Loung. *First They Killed My Father: A Daughter of Cambodia Remembers.* New York: HarperCollins, 2000.
The daughter of a high-ranking government official, Ung was only five when the Khmer Rouge stormed into Phnom Penh. This memoir tells of her family's terrible ordeal during this era and their efforts to survive.

Zéphir, Thierry. *Khmer: The Lost Empire.* New York: Harry N. Abrams, Inc., 1998.
This lushly illustrated book examines the ancient Khmer Empire and especially the magnificent temples at Angkor.

Further Reading and Websites

Ancient Cambodian Sculpture
Website: <http://www.nga.gov/exhibitions/camwel.htm>
Based on the 1997 *Sculpture of Angkor and Ancient Cambodia* exhibit at the U.S. National Gallery of Art in Washington, D.C., this site offers insights into five hundred years of Cambodian art and history.

Beauty and Darkness: The Odyssey of the Khmer People
Website: <http://www.Mekong.net/Cambodia/>
This site provides an overview of Cambodian culture and recent history, including photographs and oral histories.

Cambodia: A World of Treasures
Website: <http://www.mot.gov.kh/f_top.htm>
Run by the Cambodian Ministry of Tourism, this site offers a wealth of information about Cambodia, with specific information for visitors.

Cambodian Traditional Dance
Website: <http://www.asiasource.org/cambodia/arts.htm>
This site includes fascinating images and information about Cambodia's ancient dance tradition, along with music and links to additional sources.

Canesso, Claudia. *Cambodia*. Philadelphia: Chelsea House, 1999.
This book for young readers provides an overview of Cambodian history, culture, and geography.

De Silva, Dayaneetha, and Geraldine Mesenas. *Cambodia*. Milwaukee: Gareth Stevens, 2000.
Written for ages nine to twelve, this title offers an introduction to Cambodia, including its history, people, and government.

A Guide to the Angkor Monument
Website: <http://www.theangkorguide.com>
This fascinating website reprints the text of Maurice Glaze's classic 1944 guidebook to Angkor. The guide includes information on Khmer history, religion, architecture, and artwork, along with maps of Angkor.

Hareas, John. *Buddhism*. New York: Dorling Kindersley Publishing, 2003.
Beautifully illustrated, this book presents the rich traditions, art, and architecture of Buddhism, the dominant religion in Cambodia.

Izu, Kenro. *Passage to Angkor*. Santa Fe, NM: Channel Photographics, 2003.
This stunning book of photographs presents dramatic images of the temples at Angkor, the work of acclaimed photographer Kenro Izu. Poems accompany many of the images.

"Kingdom of Cambodia." *Royal Cambodian Embassy in Washington, D.C.* 2003.
Website: <http://www.embassy.org/cambodia/> **(October 1, 2003).**
The Cambodian embassy website offers a variety of information about the nation, with links to government and tourist information.

Levy, Debbie. *The Vietnam War.* **Minneapolis: Lerner Publications Company, 2004.**
This comprehensive title examines the causes, events, and controversies of the Vietnam War, including the U.S. bombing of Cambodia in the early 1970s.

Pastore, Clare. *Chantrea Conway's Story: A Voyage from Cambodia in 1975.* **New York: Berkley Publishing Group, 2001.**
In this novel for young readers, Chantrea's mother is killed during the terrible Khmer Rouge era. She escapes with her grandparents to Thailand, then moves to the United States, hoping to be reunited with her father.

Phnom Penh Post
Website: <http://www.phnompenhpost.com>
The paper's English-language site provides news and features about Cambodia and Cambodian life. The site is updated every two weeks.

Taus-Bolstad, Stacy. *Thailand in Pictures.* **Minneapolis: Lerner Publications Company, 2004.**
This book explores the history, culture, and society of Thailand, Cambodia's neighbor to the west. Over the centuries, the two nations have engaged in extensive trade, warfare, and cultural exchange.

—— *Vietnam in Pictures.* **Minneapolis: Lerner Publications Company, 2003.**
Vietnam is Cambodia's neighbor to the east, and the two nations have a long history of conflict. This book examines Vietnam's history, society, and culture, including its interactions with neighboring Cambodia.

vgsbooks.com
Website: <http://www.vgsbooks.com>
Visit vgsbooks.com, the homepage of the Visual Geography Series®. You can get linked to all sorts of useful on-line information, including geographical, historical, demographic, cultural, and economic websites. The vgsbooks.com site is a great resource for late-breaking news and statistics.

Captions for photos appearing on cover and chapter openers:

Cover: Huge faces of the Buddha emerge from the sandstone blocks of an Angkor Thom temple gate.

pp. 4–5 The sun rises on another steamy day at Angkor Wat.

pp. 8–9 Lush rice paddies blanket rural Cambodia.

pp. 40–41 Children gather at a roadside stand in the village of Preah Dak near the Banteay Srei temple ruins in northern Cambodia.

pp. 50–51 Dancers demonstrate the distinctive, willowy movements of a traditional dance at the Preah Kahn Temple. Complete training takes at least nine years.

pp. 60–61 Many Cambodians sell merchandise to tourists and foreign workers from market stalls, such as this one in Phnom Penh, to support their families.

Photo Acknowledgments
The images in this book are used with the permission of: © John Elk III, pp. 4–5, 7, 17, 23, 36, 42, 43, 52, 56, 60–61, 65 (left); © Digital Cartographics, pp. 6, 10; © Nevada Wier, pp. 8–9, 11, 49 (bottom); © Michele Burgess, pp. 12, 16, 25 (both); 40–41, 44, 50–51, 53 (top), 64, 65 (right); © Anders Ryman/CORBIS, p. 13; © Reuters NewMedia, Inc./CORBIS, pp. 14, 53 (bottom); © Kevin R. Morris/CORBIS, pp. 18, 49 (top); © Webistan/CORBIS, p. 19; © The Art Archive/Musée Guimet Paris/Dagli Orti, p. 22; © Bettmann/CORBIS, pp. 26, 30, 31, 34; Library of Congress, pp. 27 (LC-USZ62-96743), 29 (LC-USZ62-80580), 33 (LC-USZ62-123520); © Leonard de Selva/CORBIS, p. 28; © Brian A. Vikander, p. 35; © Reuters/Bettmann, 38; © AFP/CORBIS, pp. 45, 58; © Jim King/Photo Agora, p. 47 (top); © Bohemian Nomad Picturemakers/CORBIS, p. 47 (bottom); © Luke Golobitsh, p. 48; © Sarah Murray/Hutchison Library, p. 63; © Audrius Tomonis/www.banknotes.com, p. 68.

Cover: © Brian A. Vikander. Back cover photo: NASA.